THE
READY RESOURCE FOR

TEACHINGS OF PRESIDENTS
OF THE CHURCH

HOWARD W. HUNTER

D1603461

THE
READY RESOURCE FOR

Relief Society

TEACHINGS OF PRESIDENTS
OF THE CHURCH
HOWARD W. HUNTER

TRINA BOICE

CFI
An imprint of Cedar Fort, Inc.
Springville, Utah

ISBN 13: 978-1-4621-1749-9

Published by CFI, an imprint of Cedar Fort, Inc.
2373 W. 700 S., Springville, UT 84663
Distributed by Cedar Fort, Inc., www.cedarfort.com

Library of Congress Control Number: 2015953536

Cover design by Shawnda T. Craig
Cover design © 2015 Lyle Mortimer
Edited and typeset by Jessica B. Ellingson

Printed in the United States of America

10 9 8 7 6 5 4 3 2 1

Printed on acid-free paper

Other Books by Trina Boice

Base Hits and Home Run Relationships:
What Women Wish Guys Knew

My Future's So Bright, I Gotta Wear Shades:
An LDS Teen's Guide to Success

Dad's Night: Fantastic Family Nights in Five Minutes

The Ready Resource for Relief Society
(Six volumes)

Sabbath Solutions: More Than 350 Ways
You Can Worship on the Lord's Day

Easy Enrichment Ideas: Thinking
Outside the Green Gelatin Box

Climbing Family Trees: Whispers in the Leaves

Bright Ideas for Young Women Leaders

Great Ideas for Primary Activity Days

Parties With A Purpose: Exciting Ideas for Ward Activities

Primarily for Cub Scouts

How to Stay UP in a DOWN Economy

103 Creative Ways to Announce Your Pregnancy

A Gift of Love

Contents

Acknowledgments ix

Introduction 1

Lesson One: Jesus Christ—Our Only Way to Hope and Joy 9

Lesson Two: "My Peace I Give unto You" 15

Lesson Three: Adversity—Part of God's Plan for
Our Eternal Progress 22

Lesson Four: Help from on High 28

Lesson Five: Joseph Smith, Prophet of the Restoration 33

Lesson Six: The Atonement and Resurrection of Jesus Christ... 39

Lesson Seven: Continuous Revelation through
Living Prophets 44

Lesson Eight: Taking the Gospel to All the World 50

Lesson Nine: The Law of Tithing 57

Lesson Ten: The Scriptures—The Most Profitable
of All Study 62

Lesson Eleven: True Greatness 68

Lesson Twelve: Come Back and Feast at the
Table of the Lord 73

Lesson Thirteen: The Temple—The Great Symbol
of Our Membership 78

Lesson Fourteen: Hastening Family History
and Temple Work 83

Lesson Fifteen: The Sacrament of the Lord's Supper 88

CONTENTS

Lesson Sixteen: Marriage—An Eternal Partnership.................93

Lesson Seventeen: Preserve and Protect the Family..................98

Lesson Eighteen: We Believe in Being Honest.......................104

Lesson Nineteen: Our Commitment to God.........................109

Lesson Twenty: Walking the Savior's Path of Charity.............114

Lesson Twenty-One: Faith and Testimony 120

Lesson Twenty-Two: Teaching the Gospel 125

Lesson Twenty-Three: "No Less Serviceable" 130

Lesson Twenty-Four: Following the Example
   of Jesus Christ 135

Website Resources 143

About the Author 147

Acknowledgments

I want to thank Cedar Fort for inviting me to share this annual book series adventure with them! I also want to send a big thank you to my editor, Jessica Ellingson, for all of her help with this edition, and to marketing guru Kelly Martinez for doing such a great job of introducing my words to so many good people.

A special thanks goes to my wonderfully supportive family for taking care of everything around me while I was busy pounding away at my computer keyboard. My husband and four sons inspire me to try harder and be better every day. I'm also forever grateful for my extended family's continued enthusiastic support, unconditional love, and kind encouragement.

Thank you to all the faithful members of the Church who valiantly magnify their callings and give of their time and talents to bless those around them. Heavenly Father knows that when we teach others, we learn more deeply ourselves. They say that God loves all people, but especially teachers, because they remind Him of His Son!

Not only should we read the scriptures and have a meaningful gospel study plan, but we're commanded to *feast* on the scriptures! It is my hope that this book serves as a helpful utensil to enjoy your meal!

Introduction

President Howard W. Hunter served as President of The Church of Jesus Christ of Latter-day Saints for less than one year, yet his influence and testimony have been far-reaching. The teachings in the 2016 Relief Society and priesthood course manual come from President Hunter's sermons and articles while he served in the Church. He often used the terms *man* and *he* to refer to mankind, so help the sisters recognize that his teachings were most definitely for them too! You will enjoy helping the sisters in your ward get to know this man of God better, as well as have a desire to live the gospel with joy.

The Ready Resource for Relief Society and priesthood quorums for 2016 is designed to be a helpful, inspiring resource to make lesson preparation easier and more exciting. You can find the new Church manual for Relief Society and priesthood lessons at https://www.lds.org/manual/teachings-of-presidents-of-the-church-howard-w-hunter?lang=eng.

The gospel means "good news" and should bring us great joy! Members of The Church of Jesus Christ of Latter-day Saints should be the happiest people around! May you feel the Savior's loving arms enfold you as you teach your dear sisters and feed His sheep!

Each lesson includes hymns appropriate for the lesson, quick summaries of the lesson material, quotes to supplement your class discussions, suggested artwork to display during your presentation, and object lessons to add pizzazz to your class participation. A feature in the book that encourages your sisters to immediately apply what they learn during your lesson is the weekly challenge. Two other teaching tools that will strengthen spiritual growth and family relationships are the seminary scripture mastery verses (perfect for parents of teens), and correlating topics in the Church's *Preach My Gospel* missionary manual (perfect for parents of future and current missionaries). You're not teaching lessons—you're teaching your sisters!

A suggested handout is also provided. Each set of handouts equals the same size as half a sheet of paper, so copying is quick and easy.

The most important tool is the Holy Ghost, who will help you know how to tailor each lesson to meet the needs of your sisters.

INTRODUCTION

Teaching with the Holy Ghost is the most important tool in your class. Pray for the Holy Ghost to guide your study and preparation before your lesson and for inspiration during your lesson. As you live the commandments and do your utmost to magnify your calling, you will receive personal revelation and direction on how you should share the lessons with your sisters.

The best lessons are not lectures but rather discussions where everyone participates. Try to involve the sisters and encourage them to share their experiences and testimonies of the principles you are teaching. They should leave your class feeling edified, enriched, and excited to live the gospel with joy!

Integrating various learning styles into your lessons improves retention and attention, assists in lesson planning, and inspires participants. Everyone learns differently, so be sure to include lots of variety in your teaching techniques. Try using some of the following ideas during your lessons:

STUDENT CENTERED

Assignments	Debate
Brainstorming	Field Trip
Case Study	Games
Discussion	Panels
Instructional Games	Questions
Memorizing	Class Journal
Note Taking	Open-Ended Story
Oral Reading	Songs
Role-Playing	Crafts
Testimonies	Worksheets

TEACHER CENTERED

Jokes and Puns	Demonstration
Lecture	Surveys
Oral Reading	Catch Phrases and Tag Lines
Storytelling	Questions
Summarizing	Personal emails
Guest Speaker	Dramatization
Feedback	Personal Photos and Videos

INTRODUCTION

MATERIALS CENTERED

Bulletin Board

Chalkboard

Charts and Maps

Displays

Flash Cards

Flannel Board

DVD

Flip Chart

Overhead Transparency

Pictures and Artwork

Posters

Puppet Show

Dramatization

Social Media

Handouts

Quizzes and Tests

eBooks

Mobile Apps

Graphs

Original Films

Artwork

Comics

PowerPoint Presentations

Whiteboard

Treasure Hunt

Tape Recording

SPIRIT CENTERED

Testimony

Prayer

Scriptures

Service Projects

Building Faith

Listening for the Spirit

Temple Attendance

Devotionals

Church Standards

Love

ARTWORK

Beautiful artwork can teach in a way that words alone cannot, especially for visual learners. Your church building's library may have some larger prints of older pictures, which are numbered. Those numbers will be different than those found on pictures in the old Gospel Art Kit (KIT) that the Church used to sell in a blue box, or in the newer Gospel Art Book (GAB). Picture suggestions in this book will only include references to those two sources: KIT or GAB.

You can access many pictures on the Church's website at www.lds.org/media-library/images. There you can also find cool memes (inspirational picture quotes), desktop wallpapers to let your sisters know about, and the ever-classic Mormonads.

The pictures online are organized into almost every category you can imagine. The site now allows you to create images, as well as share your own photos and videos! Get in the habit of checking the Church's website often, because there are always new features being added.

You can purchase a Gospel Art Book (GAB) from Church Distribution at store.lds.org. It comes as a spiral-bound book containing 137 color pictures and a useful index that connects each image to the scriptures. It's an inexpensive and perfect investment for your own family home evening lessons! They are organized into the following six categories:

- Old Testament
- New Testament
- Book of Mormon
- Church History
- Gospel in Action
- Latter-day Prophets

Some terrific Church resources that provide excellent artwork on gospel themes can also be found at:

- LDS images: images.lds.org
- BYU Religious Education Image Archive: http://relarchive.byu.edu/
- Joseph Smith Resource Center (maps, artwork, photos, documents, and more!): http://josephsmith.net
- Photographs of scriptural sites: http://goo.gl/vx2SGH
- Photographs of Church History sites: http://goo.gl/z7Rtum
- Temple photos: https://goo.gl/lxQWFQ

MUSIC

Music can effectively teach and invite the Spirit almost better than any other teaching technique. Included with each lesson are suggestions for songs the class could sing or simply learn from by reading the lyrics. Inviting others in your ward to provide special musical numbers during your lessons binds hearts together and uplifts everyone. You can find the LDS hymnbook online at

- http://goo.gl/2mzPJZ

You can download songs, listen to them online, and do searches by topics, titles, and even scriptures! You can also use songs from seminary, Young Women, and Primary and other music that has been published in Church magazines. Also on the Church's website are learning materials, such as how to conduct music, how to understand symbols and terms, and where to find great ideas to add variety to singing.

Check out these great resources:

⅋ Church Hymns on iTunes: http://goo.gl/jAPwHT
⅋ Free LDS musical arrangements: http://goo.gl/CpyHLZ
⅋ Free LDS music: http://goo.gl/3Vv3H

QUOTES

Quotes from Church authorities can be used to inspire the mind and uplift the heart. It's nice to have some quotes written on the board at the front of the room for the sisters to read before class starts to set the tone and get them thinking about the topic. Some of the suggested handouts in the book use such quotes, but you can also design your own handouts with your favorite quotes. You can do a search at www.lds.org with a keyword about the topic. More can be found online at

⅋ www.quotegarden.com
⅋ www.thinkexist.com
⅋ www.inspirational-quotes.info
⅋ www.brainyquote.com
⅋ www.quotationspage.com
⅋ www.wisdomquotes.com

CHURCH MAGAZINE ARTICLES

What a blessing it is to read from Church leaders each month in the various Church magazines. Teach your class how to find material they can share with their families during family home evening lessons or to help them prepare sacrament talks in the future. Each lesson in this book includes only a few suggested articles, but there are so many more! One of the biggest blessings of preparing your lessons each month will be the focused time you get to spend researching specific gospel topics. You will learn so much more than you'll ever have time to share with your sisters in class on Sunday! Teaching Relief Society is a wonderful reason to truly immerse yourself in gospel study. Enjoy it!

Object Lessons

Object lessons capture the students' interest and increase understanding by teaching the concept in a unique way. The Savior often used physical objects that were familiar to His listeners to illustrate simple principles. Each lesson offers ideas for object lessons that could be an effective introduction to the topic or a fun way to keep the class engaged during class time.

Videos

The Church has some excellent videos that can be found and downloaded to your computer. You'll need a projector and either a white wall or screen in order to share them with your class.

A fantastic series of videos that is available online is called *The Life of Jesus Christ Bible Videos*. You can find them at www.lds.org/bible-videos, where new ones are being constantly added. You can also download a free mobile app there for viewing.

YouTube hosts several "channels" of videos officially released by the Church as well at

- http://goo.gl/qxcz8z
- http://goo.gl/Y9NqJa

You'll find a lot of other great LDS videos on YouTube that were uploaded by members of the Church. Many chapels have Internet access, but be sure to do a test run with your equipment before you decide to include videos in your lesson. Your lessons shouldn't be entertainment focused but Spirit focused.

Challenges

A meaningful addition to each lesson is the use of a personal challenge that you can share with the sisters at the end of each lesson. Perhaps it should be called an "invitation for application." The sisters need to *apply* what they've learned after they leave your classroom. If they don't *use* the lesson material to improve their lives and strengthen their testimonies, then they aren't growing spiritually from your efforts. You can offer the suggested challenge, one of your own, or invite the class to choose their own personal goal that will allow them to delve deeper and stretch farther. In the end, we won't be judged by all of the religious trivia we can recite to the Lord at the Judgment Seat, but by the Christlike qualities we have acquired. The Lord cares much more about what we are becoming than what we are doing.

Seminary Scripture Mastery

Parents of seminary students may want to learn some of the same scripture passages their teens are learning to strengthen their home and family. Teachers can mention which verses correlate with each lesson's topic. What a terrific tool it is to commit scriptures to memory together. You can see all of the seminary manuals and resources at http://goo.gl/IPVQd6.

Preach My Gospel

The Church is currently experiencing a wonderful wave of missionary service as the Lord hastens His work. To help the sisters in your ward become more familiar with this missionary service guide, consider including topical passages and talk about how to share your lesson material with nonmember friends. You can see a free copy of the manual at http://goo.gl/5u2qjs.

As a Relief Society teacher, take time to read chapter 10 in *Preach My Gospel*. Pages 175–93 offer insights on how to improve your teaching skills.

Resources

Visit the Church's website section that is dedicated to Relief Society resources under the "Serve and Teach" menu tab on the home page at www.lds.org. When you click on "Resources" you will discover all kinds of fantastic tools to help you in your sacred calling! Click on "Leadership Training Library" to see even more helpful tools. There is so much to see there.

The steps suggested for how to prepare a lesson include

- Using approved lesson materials
- Seeking the guidance of the Spirit
- Studying your lesson in advance
- Considering the needs of your sisters
- Organizing the lesson
- Seeking the gift of teaching

INTRODUCTION

Be sure to read about the life of Howard W. Hunter in the front of the 2016 Relief Society manual and share your testimony of this great prophet. The sisters will enjoy seeing pictures of him and getting to know and love him through your lessons this year.

Jesus was the Master Teacher. He still is! He cared deeply about each person He taught. He used variety, honesty, symbolism, and storytelling. He challenged His listeners to make specific changes in their lives. The more you study and teach the gospel, the greater will be your own understanding.

Use the scriptures each time you teach and encourage your class to feast from their pages. As you come to love the scriptures, your class will feel that passion and be inspired to feast upon them as well. Your task as a teacher is to invite your sisters to come unto Christ. In order to do that effectively you must create an atmosphere where the Holy Ghost will be welcome and able to testify to the hearts of your sisters.

You give voice to the gospel principles taught each week, but it is the testifying power of the Holy Ghost that touches hearts and transforms lives. May you feel the Spirit guide and direct you as you do your best to magnify this calling!

The following are articles about teaching with the Spirit:

- Henry B. Eyring, "Rise to Your Call," *Ensign,* November 2002.
- William D. Oswald, "Gospel Teaching—Our Most Important Calling," *Ensign,* November 2008.
- Dallin H. Oaks, "Gospel Teaching," *Ensign,* November 1999.
- Bruce R. McConkie, "The Teacher's Divine Commission," *Ensign,* April 1979.
- David M. McConkie, "Gospel Learning and Teaching," *Ensign,* November 2010.

Lesson One
Jesus Christ—Our Only Way to Hope and Joy

· ·

MUSIC

"Christ the Lord Is Risen Today," *Hymns* #200
"God Loved Us, So He Sent His Son," *Hymns* #187
"I Believe in Christ," *Hymns* #134
"Behold the Great Redeemer Die," *Hymns* #191
"In Humility, Our Savior," *Hymns* #172
"Our Savior's Love," *Hymns* #113

· ·

SUMMARY

Jesus Christ is the Only Begotten Son of God and the Savior of the world. He was chosen and foreordained to come to earth to atone for our sins and teach us how to return to our Heavenly Father. Our faith and hope are built upon the Savior's atoning sacrifice.

The most important event in the history of mankind was when the Savior was crucified for the world. Jesus Christ's Atonement took place in the Garden of Gethsemane and on the cross at Calvary. His redeeming sacrifice was necessary to ransom all people from the effects of sin. Because of His merciful gift, everyone has the opportunity to repent, be forgiven of their sins, and be resurrected.

To thank Him for paying our spiritual and physical debts, we must show faith in Him, repent, be baptized, and follow Him. By following Jesus Christ, we can receive peace in this life and eternal joy in the life to come. We can build a testimony of Him through scripture study, prayer, and following His example.

· ·

QUOTES

"The stories of Jesus can be like a rushing wind across the embers of faith in the hearts of our children. Jesus said, 'I am the way, the truth, and the life.' The stories of Jesus shared over and over bring faith in the Lord Jesus Christ and strength to the foundation of testimony. Can you think of a more valuable gift for our children?" (Neil L. Andersen, "Tell Me the Stories of Jesus," *Ensign*, May 2010).

"Each of you has the responsibility to know the Lord, love Him, follow Him, serve Him, teach and testify of Him" (Russell M. Nelson, "Jesus the Christ: Our Master and More," *Ensign*, April 2000).

"The soul that comes unto Christ dwells within a personal fortress, a veritable palace of perfect peace" (Jeffrey R. Holland, "Come unto Me," *Ensign*, April 1998).

"To follow Christ is to become more like Him. It is to learn from His character. As spirit children of our Heavenly Father, we do have the potential to incorporate Christlike attributes into our life and character" (Dieter F. Uchtdorf, "Christlike Attributes—the Wind beneath Our Wings," *Ensign*, November 2005).

• •

GOSPEL ART

Isaiah Writes of Christ's Birth—(113 KIT, 22 GAB)
The Birth of Jesus—(30 GAB)
The Nativity—(201 KIT)
Boy Jesus in the Temple—(205 KIT)
Childhood of Jesus Christ—(206 KIT)
John the Baptist Baptizing Jesus—(208 KIT, 35 GAB)
Calling of the Fishermen—(209 KIT, 37 GAB)
Christ Ordaining the Apostles—(211 KIT, 38 GAB)
Sermon on the Mount—(212 KIT, 39 GAB)
Christ Healing a Blind Man—(213 KIT)
Stilling the Storm—(214 KIT)
Jesus Blessing Jairus's Daughter—(215 KIT, 41 GAB)
Christ and the Children—(216 KIT, 47 GAB))
Mary and Martha—(219 KIT, 45 GAB)
Triumphal Entry—(223 KIT, 50 GAB)
Jesus Washing the Apostles' Feet—(226 KIT, 55 GAB)
Jesus Praying in Gethsemane—(227 KIT, 56 GAB)
The Betrayal of Jesus—(228 KIT)
The Crucifixion—(230 KIT, 57 GAB)
Burial of Jesus—(231 KIT, 58 GAB)

Mary and the Resurrected Lord—(233 KIT, 59 GAB)
Jesus Shows His Wounds—(234 KIT, 60 GAB)
Go Ye Therefore—(235 KIT, 61 GAB)
The Ascension of Jesus—(236 KIT, 62 GAB)
Jesus at the Door—(237 KIT, 65 GAB)
The Second Coming—(238 KIT, 66 GAB)
The Resurrected Jesus Christ—(239 KIT)
Jesus Walking on the Water—(243 KIT, 43 GAB)
Christ and the Rich Young Ruler—(244 KIT, 48 GAB)
The Empty Tomb—(245 KIT)
Jesus Teaching in the Western Hemisphere—(315 KIT, 82 GAB)
Christ and Children from around the World—(608 KIT)
Jesus Blesses the Nephite Children—(84 GAB)

VIDEOS

- There are many videos to choose from in the Church's new Bible Videos about the life of Jesus Christ found at https://goo.gl/BmBrXc
- "Jesus Declares He Is the Messiah": https://goo.gl/o9tIDv
- "Are We Christians?": https://goo.gl/CAuMnc
- See some of the great testimonies of Christ on www.mormonchannel.org/watch/series under "I'm a Mormon," "Bible Videos," and "New Testament Stories"

OBJECT LESSONS

- Show various objects and ask how they relate to Jesus Christ:
  - Porch light: serves as a beacon to help us find our way home
  - Campfire: provides warmth and comfort
  - Lighthouse: Offers light in the darkness and offers perspective in the storm
  - Nightlight: banishes darkness and eliminates fear
  - Car headlights: lets us know where we are heading
  - Lights in a movie theater: a guide that can be followed
  - Lightbulb: inspires us and brings us new light and understanding

❧ Display a beautiful rose, but with the thorns still intact. Talk about how fragrant and pleasing it is. Next, bruise some of the rose petals and point out the thorns. Jesus's body was bruised for our iniquities and a crown of thorns was placed on his head. Now ask someone to be a timekeeper and someone else to take the rose petals off the stem as fast as possible. Ask for another volunteer and timekeeper. Say, "Okay, let's see if you can beat that time. Ready? Put it back together!" No matter how hard we try, we can't rebuild a rose. Not only can God do that, but He can also restore life through Jesus Christ. We are even more beautiful than a rose and will all be resurrected, because with God, all things are possible!

❧ Ask for a volunteer to stand in a square that is marked on the floor with masking tape. Show her a candy bar on the table and tell her she can have it only if she can reach it without leaving the square. Ask for another volunteer to help her. That's what the Savior does for us: He bridges the gap between mortality and eternal life. His Atonement gives us the gift of repentance so we taste the sweet love of Heavenly Father!

❧ Ask someone in the class to put on a sock. Hand the volunteer a muddy sock. The volunteer will probably not want to touch the dirty sock, so ask her what could be done to make her willing. Tell her you'll take the muddy sock and give her a new clean one. The Savior took upon Himself all of our dirty sins and gave us each a clean sock to wear when we return to our Father in Heaven, so that we will be clean from the sins of the world.

❧ Set out pictures of the Savior around the room. Invite sisters to select one and talk about it. The sisters' comments will likely turn into sweet testimonies about the Savior.

❧ See more ideas in Lesson Six.

• •

CHURCH MAGAZINE ARTICLES

❧ Ezra Taft Benson, "Five Marks of the Divinity of Jesus Christ," *Ensign*, December 2001.

❧ Ezra Taft Benson, "Jesus Christ: Our Savior and Redeemer," *Ensign*, June 1990.

ﻌ Russell M. Nelson, "Jesus the Christ: Our Master and More,"
Ensign, April 2000.

ﻌ Orson F. Whitney, "The Divinity of Jesus Christ," *Ensign*,
December 2003.

• •

CHALLENGE

Write your testimony of Jesus Christ in your journal and share it
with your family. Write it in a Book of Mormon and share it with a
nonmember.

• •

SEMINARY SCRIPTURE MASTERY

Helaman 5:12   Genesis 1:26–27
Isaiah 53:3–5   Matthew 16:15–19
Luke 24:36–39   John 3:5
John 17:3   1 Corinthians 15:20–22
D&C 19:16–19   D&C 76:22–24
D&C 130:22–23

• •

PREACH MY GOSPEL

Pages 34, 36–37, 47–48, 51–52, 60–62, 90, 105, 115–26

• •

"To follow Christ is to become more like Him."

Dieter F. Uchtdorf, "Christlike Attributes—the Wind beneath Our Wings," *Ensign*, November 2005

"To follow Christ is to become more like Him."

Dieter F. Uchtdorf, "Christlike Attributes—the Wind beneath Our Wings," *Ensign*, November 2005

Lesson Two
"My Peace I Give unto You"

● ●

MUSIC

"Before Thee, Lord, I Bow My Head," *Hymns* #158
"Sweet Hour of Prayer," *Hymns* #142
"A Child's Prayer," *Children's Songbook* #12
"Joseph Smith's First Prayer," *Hymns* #26
"O God, Our Help in Ages Past," *Hymns* #31
"For the Strength of the Hills," *Hymns* #35
"Awake, Ye Saints of God, Awake!" *Hymns* #17
"Cast Thy Burden upon the Lord," *Hymns* #110
"Come, All Ye Saints of Zion," *Hymns* #38

● ●

SUMMARY

These are the last days! We have much to do to prepare the world for the Savior's Second Coming. Wickedness is increasing at an ever-rapid pace, and our homes and values are being assaulted on every side. Still, the positive influence members of the Church can have on those around them can be powerful if we are not afraid to stand as witnesses of Christ. We can help the pure in heart feel secure as we offer them an anchor against the storms howling around us. Christ told us to "be of good cheer; I have overcome the world" (John 16:33).

Relief Society sisters need to be courageous to step into their communities and be an influence for good. The gospel of Jesus Christ is the only thing that will bring peace to the world; the Prince of Peace is the answer to the earth's woes. We can prevent the adversary from having any power over our homes and hearts by obeying the Lord's commandments, which have been designed to protect us. We can look for the good and be positive about all of the wonderful blessings we have. We don't have to wait until the Lord comes again to feel joy.

● ●

QUOTES

"Even with the trials of life, because of the Savior's Atonement and His grace, righteous living will be rewarded with personal peace" (Quentin L. Cook, "Personal Peace: The Reward of Righteousness," *Ensign*, May 2013).

"God expects you to have enough faith, determination, and trust in Him to keep moving, keep living, keep rejoicing. . . . He expects you to embrace and shape the future—to love it, rejoice in it, and delight in your opportunities" (Jeffrey R. Holland, "This, the Greatest of All Dispensations," *Ensign*, July 2007).

"Ancient prophets looked with enthusiastic anticipation to our dispensation when the fulness of the gospel would be restored and preached among all nations, and when final preparations would be made for the Second Coming and ultimate reign of the King of Kings, our Savior. Great eternal blessings, keys, and secrets of the gospel, which have been kept 'hid from before the foundation of the world,' were reserved to come forth in this final dispensation to bless our lives. How privileged we are to live in these momentous times!" (J. Lewis Taylor, "I Have a Question: How shall I read the parables of preparation in Matthew 25 in the context of the last days?" *Ensign*, June 1975).

"These are the last days. As has been foretold by God's holy prophets since the world began, they are challenging times, and they are going to become even more challenging. . . . [Satan's] sole purpose is to make you and me as miserable as he is, and the best way for him to accomplish that is to entice us into disobedience. Although there are all kinds of misery in this world, the only kind that is eternal is misery of the soul. And that kind of misery is centered in sin and transgression" (M. Russell Ballard, "When Shall These Things Be?" *Ensign*, December 1996).

"Paul, in describing our 'perilous times,' did not promise that things would necessarily get easier or necessarily better. He did give counsel to those seeking comfort and assurance in the face of the deteriorating conditions of our day. Just as his prophecies or predictions were clearly accurate, so is his direction to us remarkably relevant as well. Said he, 'Continue . . . in the things which thou hast learned

and hast been assured of, knowing of whom thou hast learned them'"
(Cecil O. Samuelson Jr., "Perilous Times," *Ensign,* November 2004).

"Our Father in Heaven has promised us peace in times of trial and
has provided a way for us to come to Him in our need. He has given
us the privilege and power of prayer" (Rex D. Pinegar, "Peace through
Prayer," *Ensign,* May 1993).

• •

GOSPEL ART

Noah and the Ark with Animals—(103 KIT, 8 GAB)
Daniel Refusing the King's Meat and Wine—(114 KIT, 23 GAB)
Three Men in the Fiery Furnace—(116 KIT, 25 GAB)
Daniel in the Lions' Den—(117 KIT, 26 GAB)
Flight into Egypt—(204 KIT)
The Betrayal of Jesus—(228 KIT)
Lehi Prophesying to the People of Jerusalem—(300 KIT, 67 GAB)
Abinadi before King Noah—(308 KIT, 75 GAB)
Alma Baptizes in the Waters of Mormon—(309 KIT, 76 GAB)
Ammon Defends the Flocks of King Lamoni—(310 KIT, 78 GAB)
The Anti-Nephi-Lehies Burying Their Swords—(311 KIT)
Captain Moroni Raises the Title of Liberty—(312 KIT, 79 GAB)
Two Thousand Young Warriors—(313 KIT, 80 GAB)
Samuel the Lamanite on the Wall—(314 KIT, 81 GAB)
Mormon Bids Farewell to a Once Great Nation—(319 KIT)
Saving the Book of Commandments—(409 KIT)
Helping the Martin Handcart Company across the Sweetwater
    River—(415 KIT)
Salt Lake Temple—(502 KIT, 119 GAB)
Washington DC Temple—(505 KIT)
Latter-day Prophets—(506–22 KIT, 122–37 GAB)
Passing the Sacrament—(108 GAB)
Young Boy Praying—(605 KIT, 111 GAB)
Family Prayer—(606 KIT, 112 GAB)
Young Couple Going to the Temple—(609 KIT, 120 GAB)
Search the Scriptures—(617 KIT)
My Gospel Standards—(619 KIT)
Jesus Praying in Gethsemane—(227 KIT, 56 GAB)

Enos Praying—(305 KIT, 72 GAB)
The First Vision—(403 KIT, 90 GAB)

• •

VIDEOS

- ❧ "Be Not Troubled": https://goo.gl/7Xu8lE
- ❧ "They that are Wise": https://goo.gl/ky9yp8
- ❧ "Watchmen on the Tower": https://goo.gl/UQW0UI
- ❧ "The Whole Armor of God": https://goo.gl/ZkkZ9p
- ❧ "Seek and Attain the Spiritual High Ground in Life": https://goo.gl/rNqyNo
- ❧ "Pray Often": https://goo.gl/v0Ngkf
- ❧ "And My Soul Hungered": https://goo.gl/lS6wfa

• •

OBJECT LESSONS

- ❧ Ask the class how many of them like to eat cake. Have them list the ingredients in the cake and ask if they like to eat the raw ingredients separately. Explain that it's a lot like life: separately there are some bitter times, some raw and hurtful times, and some dry and bland times. But there are also good times! Together, God is able to blend them all together to create a life that is meaningful, useful, and tasty! Read Romans 8:28: "All things work together for good to them that love God, to them who are the called according to his purpose." The Lord has warned us that perilous times are coming, but they are part of the plan. We need to continue to be righteous and know that He has the best recipe. Pass out pieces of cake to enjoy!
- ❧ Matthew 5:13 reads, "Ye are the salt of the earth: but if the salt have lost his savour, wherewith shall it be salted? it is thenceforth good for nothing, but to be cast out, and to be trodden under foot of men." Explain that we are the salt of the earth and that it's pretty easy for us to lose our flavor if we don't attend Church, pray, or study the scriptures. Place a salt shaker on the edge of a lazy Susan. Spin it slowly at first and then fast enough that the salt shaker falls off. The perilous days in which we live are represented by the spinning increasing in speed. Now place the salt shaker in

18

the center of the lazy Susan. When you spin it, the salt won't fall off. We need to be centered in Christ in order to withstand the difficult times that are ahead. Eat something salty and be happy!

꽃 See the object lessons in Lesson Three.

꽃 Show the class a silver tray that is tarnished and ask if they know how silver is made. Explain that silver has to be refined. In order to do that, the silversmith holds a piece of silver over a fire and lets it heat up. The silver must be held in the middle of the fire where the flames are the hottest to burn away all the impurities. Malachi 3:3 describes God as a refiner and purifier of silver. Sometimes in life it may seem to us that God is holding us in a "hot spot." When a silversmith does this, he never leaves. He sits in front of the fire and watches the silver very carefully. He knows that if the silver is left even a moment too long in the flames, it will be destroyed. God may allow things to come into our lives to help purify us, but He will never leave us too long and let us be destroyed. He is with us and always carefully watching. So how does the silversmith know when the silver is purified? It's when he can see his image in it. The Lord needs to refine us so we can become like Him! These last days will be a purifying time for His Saints who will have the privilege of seeing Him return to the earth in glory.

CHURCH MAGAZINE ARTICLES

꽃 Richard G. Scott, "The Sustaining Power of Faith in Times of Uncertainty and Testing," *Ensign,* May 2003.

꽃 Cecil O. Samuelson Jr., "Perilous Times," *Ensign,* November 2004.

꽃 George P. Lee, "Staying Unspotted from the World," *Ensign,* May 1978.

꽃 Boyd K. Packer, "The Test," *Ensign,* November 2008.

꽃 L. Tom Perry, "The Tradition of a Balanced, Righteous Life," *Ensign,* August 2011.

꽃 James E. Faust, "The Lifeline of Prayer," *Ensign,* May 2002.

CHALLENGE

All we have to do is read the news headlines to feel depressed or overwhelmed. Focus on the positive by writing a list of all the good things happening in the world, in the Church, and in your life today. Begin a gratitude journal where you record the good, happy, and joyful moments of each day.

SEMINARY SCRIPTURE MASTERY

1 Nephi 3:7	2 Nephi 2:25
Alma 32:21	Alma 41:10
Ether 12:6	Moroni 7:45, 47–48
Proverbs 3:5–6	Isaiah 53:3–5
Malachi 4:5–6	2 Thessalonians 2:1–3
D&C 18:10	D&C 18:15–16
D&C 25:13	D&C 64:23

PREACH MY GOSPEL

Pages 38, 50, 66, 73, 88, 97–99, 118, 124–26, 168–69

"Even with the trials of life, because of the Savior's Atonement and His grace, righteous living will be rewarded with personal peace."

Quentin L. Cook, "Personal Peace: The Reward of Righteousness," *Ensign*, May 2013

"Even with the trials of life, because of the Savior's Atonement and His grace, righteous living will be rewarded with personal peace."

Quentin L. Cook, "Personal Peace: The Reward of Righteousness," *Ensign*, May 2013

Lesson Three
Adversity—Part of God's Plan
for Our Eternal Progress

. . . .

Music

"Choose the Right," *Hymns* #239
"I Will Follow God's Plan," *Children's Songbook* #164
"Arise, O Glorious Zion," *Hymns* #40
"Cast Thy Burden upon the Lord," *Hymns* #110
"Come, All Ye Saints of Zion," *Hymns* #38
"Glorious Things Are Sung of Zion," *Hymns* #48
"How Firm a Foundation," *Hymns* #85
"I Need My Heavenly Father," *Children's Songbook* #18

. . . .

Summary

By following Jesus Christ, we are choosing eternal life and liberty. If we follow Satan, we are selecting evil and eternal captivity. One of the purposes of mortality for us is to show what choices we'll make, and so there must be opposition in all things for us to exercise agency.

The trials and tribulations we face will help us grow spiritually, will refine us, and will build our Christlike character. Adversity is designed to be a part of our earthly life experience to strengthen our physical and spiritual muscles. So rather than question, "Why me?" we should ask, "What can I learn from this experience?"

Our trials are designed to soften our hearts and bring us closer to Christ. We need not fear or lose hope. Following the Savior will ease our burdens and lighten our loads. He has overcome the world and wants to help us do the same.

. . . .

Quotes

"Repeated assurances have been given regarding the benefits and blessings of positive responses to adversity, however undeserved. The witness of the Spirit and the manifestation of greater things often follow the trial of one's faith. Spiritual refinement may be realized in the furnace of affliction. Thereby we may be prepared to experience personal and direct contact with God" (Ronald E. Poelman, "Adversity and the Divine Purpose of Mortality," *Ensign*, May 1989).

"While the freedom to choose involves the risk of mistakes, it also offers the opportunity, through our Father's plan, to overcome them" (Spencer J. Condie, "Agency: The Gift of Choices," *Ensign*, September 1995).

"Rather than simply passing through trials, we must allow trials to pass through us in ways that sanctify us" (Neal A. Maxwell, "Enduring Well," *Ensign*, April 1997).

"We cannot expect to learn endurance in our later years if we have developed the habit of quitting when things get difficult now" (Robert D. Hales, "Behold, We Count Them Happy Which Endure," *Ensign*, May 1998).

"Paul, in describing our 'perilous times,' did not promise that things would necessarily get easier or necessarily better. He did give counsel to those seeking comfort and assurance in the face of the deteriorating conditions of our day. Just as his prophecies or predictions were clearly accurate, so is his direction to us remarkably relevant as well. Said he, 'Continue . . . in the things which thou hast learned and hast been assured of, knowing of whom thou hast learned them'" (Cecil O. Samuelson Jr., "Perilous Times," *Ensign*, November 2004).

• •

GOSPEL ART

Ruth Gleaning in the Fields—(17 GAB)
Building the Ark—(102 KIT, 7 GAB)
The Good Samaritan—(218 KIT, 44 GAB)
Parable of the Ten Virgins—(53 GAB)
Jesus at the Door—(237 KIT, 65 GAB)
Lehi's Dream—(69 GAB)
Enos Praying—(305 KIT, 72 GAB)
Captain Moroni Raises the Title of Liberty—(312 KIT, 79 GAB)
Two Thousand Young Warriors—(313 KIT, 80 GAB)
Emma Crossing the Ice—(96 GAB)
The Foundation of the Relief Society—(98 GAB)

Handcart Pioneers Approaching the Salt Lake Valley—(414 KIT, 102 GAB)

Service—(115 GAB)

Noah and the Ark with Animals—(103 KIT, 8 GAB)

Three Men in the Fiery Furnace—(116 KIT, 25 GAB)

Daniel in the Lions' Den—(117 KIT, 26 GAB)

Flight into Egypt—(204 KIT)

Abinadi before King Noah—(308 KIT, 75 GAB)

Samuel the Lamanite on the Wall—(314 KIT, 81 GAB)

Helping the Martin Handcart Company across the Sweetwater River—(415 KIT)

Joseph Smith in Liberty Jail—(97 GAB)

• •

VIDEOS

❧ "Be Not Troubled": goo.gl/7Xu8lE

❧ Julie Beck, "Trials and Adversity": http://goo.gl/cjFkqm

❧ Shauna Ewing, "Enduring It Well": http://goo.gl/ehB3FC

❧ "Come What May and Love It": https://goo.gl/QJiX8Y

• •

OBJECT LESSONS

❧ Set up a game of Jenga, Stack Attack, or a simple stack of wooden blocks in a weave pattern where you pull out the blocks and re-stack them on top until the tower tumbles. Invite class members to remove one of the blocks and mention a trial that can occur in our lives, as well as a strength we gain when we successfully triumph over the challenge. Eventually, the tower will fall. So will our spirituality when we lose hope or stop following the Savior. We don't always have the power to select our trails, but we always have the freedom to choose how we will respond to them.

❧ Show the class a piece of sandpaper and explain that it is carefully designed to not be too rough but just rough enough to make a piece of wood smoother. This is similar to how the Lord allows us to be tested or tried in our lives—not beyond what we can bear. He does this to make us stronger and more refined (see 1 Corinthians 10:13; James 1:2–4).

- See the object lessons in Lesson Two.
- Have the class stand up and ask them to jump as high as they can, but with the stipulation that they can't bend their knees. (They won't be able to jump very high.) Now instruct them to jump again, but this time they can bend their knees as low as they want before launching upward. Point out to them that the only way to reach and jump high is to bend low first. When we are brought low with trials or difficulties, we must remember that it takes that bending low to propel us higher. If we are brought low with trials, then we can build sufficient faith and trust in God so He can lift us to a higher spiritual place.

Church Magazine Articles

- Richard G. Scott, "The Sustaining Power of Faith in Times of Uncertainty and Testing," *Ensign,* May 2003.
- Cecil O. Samuelson Jr., "Perilous Times," *Ensign*, November 2004.
- Boyd K. Packer, "The Test," *Ensign*, November 2008.
- Neal A. Maxwell, "Enduring Well," *Ensign,* April 1997.

Challenge

Each day is filled with challenges and problems to overcome. Sometimes we create our own problems by making bad choices, but often we are placed in difficult circumstances for other reasons not of our own doing. Write a list of the trials in your life and the Christlike qualities you can develop as you endure and overcome them.

Seminary Scripture Mastery

1 Nephi 3:7	2 Nephi 2:27
2 Nephi 28:7–9	Mosiah 3:19
Mosiah 4:30	Alma 41:10
Helaman 5:12	Moroni 7:45
Exodus 20:3–17	Isaiah 1:18
John 14:15	Revelation 20:12–13

D&C 1:37–38   D&C 14:7
D&C 58:27

• •

PREACH MY GOSPEL

Pages 47–50, 66, 72, 75, 150–51

• •

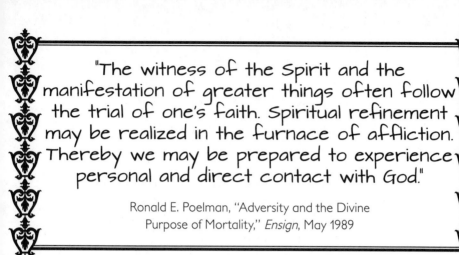

"The witness of the Spirit and the manifestation of greater things often follow the trial of one's faith. Spiritual refinement may be realized in the furnace of affliction. Thereby we may be prepared to experience personal and direct contact with God."

Ronald E. Poelman, "Adversity and the Divine Purpose of Mortality," *Ensign*, May 1989

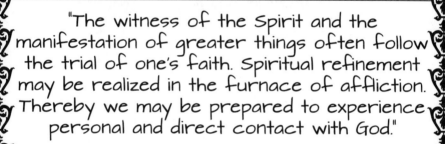

"The witness of the Spirit and the manifestation of greater things often follow the trial of one's faith. Spiritual refinement may be realized in the furnace of affliction. Thereby we may be prepared to experience personal and direct contact with God."

Ronald E. Poelman, "Adversity and the Divine Purpose of Mortality," *Ensign*, May 1989

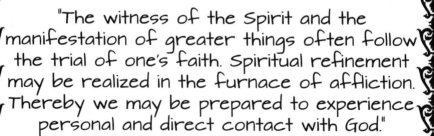

"The witness of the Spirit and the manifestation of greater things often follow the trial of one's faith. Spiritual refinement may be realized in the furnace of affliction. Thereby we may be prepared to experience personal and direct contact with God."

Ronald E. Poelman, "Adversity and the Divine Purpose of Mortality," *Ensign*, May 1989

Lesson Four
Help from on High

Music

"Before Thee, Lord, I Bow My Head," *Hymns* #158
"Did You Think to Pray?" *Hymns* #140
"Prayer Is the Soul's Sincere Desire," *Hymns* #145
"Sweet Hour of Prayer," *Hymns* #142
"A Child's Prayer," *Children's Songbook* #12
"O God, Our Help in Ages Past," *Hymns* #31
"For the Strength of the Hills," *Hymns* #35
"Cast Thy Burden upon the Lord," *Hymns* #110

• •

Summary

One of the most powerful truths we can know is that the Creator of the universe knows and loves us personally. Prayer enables us to talk to our Father who is in heaven as if He were speaking with us face to face here on earth. How wonderful it is not only that God truly hears our prayers, but that He wants to hear them. Inspired lives include daily personal prayer, family prayer, and, if we are married, companionship prayer. Those prayers should be filled with active listening. God answers our prayers by granting us increased ability or by inspiring others to help us. As we pray, we draw closer to our Heavenly Father until our will is the same as His.

We can also receive help from on high by studying the scriptures. We increase our ability to receive personal inspiration when we take time to pray, study the scriptures, ponder, and listen to promptings from the Holy Ghost.

• •

Quotes

"Perhaps no promise in life is more reassuring than that promise of divine assistance and spiritual guidance in times of need. It is a gift freely given from heaven, a gift that we need from our earliest youth through the very latest days of our lives" (Howard W. Hunter "Blessed from on High," *Ensign*, November 1988).

"Prayer is a supernal gift of our Father in Heaven to every soul. Think of it: the absolute Supreme Being, the most all-knowing, all-seeing, all-powerful personage, encourages you and me, as insignificant as we are, to converse with Him as our Father. . . . A key to improved prayer is to learn to ask the right questions. Consider changing from asking for the things you want to honestly seeking what He wants for you. Then as you learn His will, pray that you will be led to have the strength to fulfill it" (Richard G. Scott, "Using the Supernal Gift of Prayer," *Ensign*, May 2007).

"Our Father in Heaven has promised us peace in times of trial and has provided a way for us to come to Him in our need. He has given us the privilege and power of prayer" (Rex D. Pinegar, "Peace through Prayer," *Ensign*, May 1993).

"Men and women of integrity, character, and purpose have ever recognized a power higher than themselves and have sought through prayer to be guided by such power" (Thomas S. Monson, "The Prayer of Faith," *Ensign*, August 1995).

Gospel Art

Jesus Praying in Gethsemane—(227 KIT, 56 GAB)
Enos Praying—(305 KIT, 72 GAB)
Moroni Hides the Plates in the Hill Cumorah—(320 KIT, 86 GAB)
The First Vision—(403 KIT, 90 GAB)
Young Boy Praying—(605 KIT, 111 GAB)
Family Prayer—(606 KIT, 112 GAB)
Daniel in the Lions' Den—(117 KIT, 26 GAB)
Daniel Refusing the King's Meat and Wine—(114 KIT, 23 GAB)
Three Men in the Fiery Furnace—(116 KIT, 25 GAB)
Search the Scriptures—(617 KIT)

Videos

- "Pray Often": https://goo.gl/v0Ngkf
- "Pray in Your Families": https://goo.gl/X6gNbl

❧ "Pray with Faith": https://goo.gl/ypvj24
❧ "And My Soul Hungered": https://goo.gl/lS6wfa
❧ "How God Talks to Us Today": https://goo.gl/La8MMc

• •

OBJECT LESSONS

❧ Invite the class to share their experiences of trying to find a moment in their hectic lives for personal prayer. Before the discussion, ask a volunteer in private to keep raising her hand while you ignore her. You could even acknowledge her but tell her you need to say a few more things before she can talk. Finally, when you call on her, have her tell the class of your plan and explain that sometimes our prayers are like that: we do all of the talking and don't let the Lord participate in the discussion!

❧ As you walk into the room, talk loudly on your mobile phone as if you are talking to a friend. Talk about your plans for the day and the things you need to do and then ask for advice as though you are talking to a good friend. Ask the class to compare your conversation to prayer. Remind them that talking on a cellphone is different from prayer in the following ways:
  • God is never out of range
  • We never lose the signal
  • The battery never dies
  • We never run out of minutes
  • We don't have to remember God's number. Just talk!

❧ Show a letter that is addressed to someone but doesn't have a postage stamp on it and ask the class why the postman won't deliver it. Read Alma 33:11 and ask why the prayer of Zenos was heard? Explain that the postage stamp represents sincerity. Sincerity is the postage that delivers our letter (prayer) to Heavenly Father.

❧ Ask the class to take several long, deep breaths. There are interesting breathing exercises you can find online that you could have the sisters do for a few minutes. We need to breathe to stay alive. When we breathe, we inhale oxygen and exhale carbon dioxide. Breathing actually cleanses us. Just as breathing can bring cleansing to our physical bodies, so prayer can to our spiritual bodies. Prayer can be a lot like breathing. We need to pray to stay

30

spiritually alive. Paul states in 1 Thessalonians 5:17 that we are to "pray without ceasing." We can't live if we cease breathing. We need to connect with God in prayer. It is essential to our spiritual health and survival!

· ·

Church Magazine Articles

❧ David A. Bednar, "Pray Always," *Ensign*, November 2008.
❧ Dallin H. Oaks, "The Language of Prayer," *Ensign*, May 1993.
❧ Russell M. Nelson, "Lessons from the Lord's Prayers," *Ensign*, May 2009.
❧ James E. Faust, "The Lifeline of Prayer," *Ensign*, May 2002.
❧ N. Eldon Tanner, "Importance and Efficacy of Prayer," *Ensign*, August 1971.
❧ Spencer W. Kimball, "Pray Always," *Ensign*, October 1981.

· ·

Challenge

Say a prayer today without asking for anything; just give thanks to the Lord. Offer another prayer tomorrow, focusing on other people's needs and how you could help them. Don't mention any of your needs. (Heavenly Father already knows about them anyway!) Write in your journal about those two conversations with Heavenly Father.

· ·

Seminary Scripture Mastery

2 Nephi 32:8–9   James 1:5–6
D&C 8:2–3   D&C 10:5
D&C 25:13

· ·

Preach My Gospel

Pages 39, 73, 93–95

· ·

"Perhaps no promise in life is more reassuring than that promise of divine assistance and spiritual guidance in times of need. It is a gift freely given from heaven, a gift that we need from our earliest youth through the very latest days of our lives."

Howard W. Hunter, "Blessed from on High," *Ensign*, November 1988

"Perhaps no promise in life is more reassuring than that promise of divine assistance and spiritual guidance in times of need. It is a gift freely given from heaven, a gift that we need from our earliest youth through the very latest days of our lives."

Howard W. Hunter, "Blessed from on High," *Ensign*, November 1988

Lesson Five

Joseph Smith, Prophet
of the Restoration

● ●

MUSIC

"An Angel Came to Joseph Smith," *Children's Songbook* #86
"Come, Listen to a Prophet's Voice," *Hymns* #21
"Joseph Smith's First Prayer," *Hymns* #26
"Praise to the Man," *Hymns* #27
"Truth Eternal," *Hymns* #4

● ●

SUMMARY

Every member of the Church has to decide for herself what she believes about the Prophet Joseph, since it is the pivotal point of our religion. Every member can find out by doing what Joseph did—going to the Lord in earnest, sincere prayer. By studying and praying about the truthfulness of the Book of Mormon, the fruit of Joseph Smith's ministry, we can know if he truly was a prophet of the Lord sent to restore the fulness of the gospel in these latter days.

Through Joseph Smith, all the keys and ordinances required for our salvation were restored to earth. Through Joseph's experiences and writings, we have a greater understanding of the nature of God and our relationship to Him. The Prophet Joseph was called to stand at the head of this dispensation and seal his testimony with his blood. The young prophet gave his life for his testimony of the Savior; we should be willing to live our lives, testifying to others about what happened in that sacred grove of trees and in our own hearts.

● ●

QUOTES

"Through Joseph Smith have been restored all the powers, keys, teachings, and ordinances necessary for salvation and exaltation" (Tad R. Callister, "Joseph Smith—Prophet of the Restoration," *Ensign*, November 2009).

"Joseph Smith the Prophetwas the chosen instrument through which the Restoration took place" (Rex C. Reeve, "Joseph Smith, the Chosen Instrument," *Ensign*, November 1985).

"Bonds and imprisonments and persecutions are no disgrace to the Saints. It is that that is common in all ages of the world since the days of Adam. . . . The same things produce the same effect in every age of the world. We only want the same patience, the same carefulness, the same guide, the same grace, the same faith in our Lord Jesus Christ. . . . What we do not learn by precept we may learn by experience. All these things are to make us wise and intelligent that we may be the happy recipients of the highest glory" (Hyrum Smith, Church Patriarch, 1841–44, Letter to Mary Fielding Smith, ca. 1839, probably from Liberty Jail, Liberty, Missouri, Church Archives, The Church of Jesus Christ of Latter-day Saints, Salt Lake City, Utah; spelling, punctuation, and capitalization modernized).

"No testimony is more significant to us in our time than the witness of Joseph Smith. He was the prophet chosen to restore the ancient Church of Christ in this, the last time when the gospel will be on the earth before the return of Jesus Christ. Like all the prophets who opened the work of God in their dispensations, Joseph was given especially clear and powerful prophetic experiences to prepare the world for the Savior's Second Coming" (Robert D. Hales, "Seeking to Know God, Our Heavenly Father, and His Son, Jesus Christ," *Ensign*, November 2009).

"The more I know of the Prophet Joseph, the more I love him, the more I yearn to follow his example, the more I appreciate what our Father in Heaven and His Son have done in restoring this gospel that is destined to fill the earth in these, the latter days" (Joseph B. Wirthlin, "Growing into the Priesthood," *Ensign*, November 1999).

"Like Joseph, we must search the scriptures and pray. For many, this means overcoming feelings of doubt and unworthiness, being humble, and learning to exercise faith" (Robert D. Hales, "Receiving a Testimony of the Restored Gospel of Jesus Christ," *Ensign*, November 2003).

• •

Gospel Art

The Bible and Book of Mormon: Two Witnesses—(326 KIT)
The Prophet Joseph Smith—(401 KIT, 122 GAB)
Joseph Smith Seeks Wisdom in the Bible—(402 KIT, 89 GAB)
The First Vision—(403 KIT, 90 GAB)
Moroni Appears to Joseph Smith in His Room—(404 KIT, 91 GAB)
Joseph Smith Receives the Gold Plates—(406 KIT)
John the Baptist Conferring the Aaronic Priesthood—(407 KIT, 93 GAB)
Melchizedek Priesthood Restoration—(408 KIT, 94 GAB)
Translating the Book of Mormon—(416 KIT, 92 GAB)
Elijah Appearing in the Kirkland Temple—(417 KIT, 95 GAB)
Latter-day Prophets—(506–22 KIT, 122–37 GAB)

• •

Videos

❧ "Joseph Smith: Prophet of the Restoration": https://goo.gl/Ngil5s
❧ "Joseph Smith Papers": https://goo.gl/jX3K5n
❧ "The Apostasy and the Restoration—What the Restoration Means for Me": https://goo.gl/Mi8LVk
❧ "Joseph Smith Commemorative Broadcast": https://goo.gl/IAbHdm
❧ "The Message of the Restoration": https://goo.gl/2mEHrr

• •

Object Lessons

❧ Take apart a flashlight and give some of the pieces to different sisters in the class. Ask them to shine the light. They won't be able to because they don't have all the parts. Now put the pieces together and ask a volunteer to shine the light. Explain how Joseph Smith was given the fulness of the gospel to shine brightly in the world. All of the churches that existed were good, like the pieces of the flashlight, but the full gospel light couldn't shine until they were given to Joseph Smith.
❧ Tell the class you're going to show pictures of different kinds of cars and they should raise their hands when they see a car that represents the kind of person they are (sports car, truck, minivan,

race car, luxury sedan, taxi, and so on). Explain that all cars get old and eventually break down. Age, accidents, and everyday use will wear a car out. Sooner or later, all cars are destined for the junkyard unless someone restores them. In some ways, our lives are like the cars. Just as all cars break down, all people can wear out and die spiritually. Just as a car can't fix its own dent or flat tires, we can't fix all the problems in our lives. The Savior keeps our cars running in good condition. He sends auto mechanics (prophets) who know how to restore cars to their best state when they get old and rusty. Joseph restored the Church after the Great Apostasy.

⅜ Invite someone to play a hymn or song on the piano, but tape down most of the piano keys. After the deaths of the early Apostles, God's authority and the fulness of the gospel was lost to the earth. Explain that there are many wonderful churches on earth today that have some of the piano keys to enjoy, but The Church of Jesus Christ of Latter-day Saints allows us to enjoy the whole song as it was intended—the fulness of the gospel. Joseph Smith was an instrument in the Lord's hands.

. . . .

Church Magazine Articles

⅜ Dallin H Oaks, "Joseph, the Man and the Prophet," *Ensign*, May 1996.

⅜ Gordon B. Hinckley, "What Hath God Wrought through His Servant Joseph!" *Ensign*, May 1980.

⅜ Neal A. Maxwell, "The Wondrous Restoration," *Ensign*, April 2003.

⅜ Charles Didier, "The Message of the Restoration," *Ensign*, November 2003.

. . . .

Challenge

Read some of the Joseph Smith papers at www.JosephSmithPapers. org or watch the video presentations about them at LDS.org

. . . .

Seminary Scripture Mastery

Helaman 5:12	Isaiah 29:13–14
Amos 3:7	2 Timothy 3:15–17
James 1:5–6	Joseph Smith—History 1:15–20
D&C 1:37–38	D&C 76:22–24

• •

Preach My Gospel

Pages 6–7, 32–33, 35–37

• •

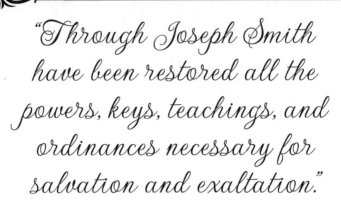

"Through Joseph Smith have been restored all the powers, keys, teachings, and ordinances necessary for salvation and exaltation."

Tad R. Callister, "Joseph Smith—Prophet of the Restoration," *Ensign*, November 2009

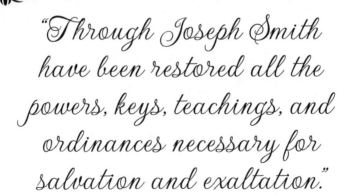

"Through Joseph Smith have been restored all the powers, keys, teachings, and ordinances necessary for salvation and exaltation."

Tad R. Callister, "Joseph Smith—Prophet of the Restoration," *Ensign*, November 2009

Lesson Six
The Atonement and Resurrection of Jesus Christ

MUSIC

> "Christ The Lord Is Risen Today," *Hymns* #200
> "God Loved Us, So He Sent His Son" *Hymns* #187
> "I Believe in Christ," *Hymns* #134
> "Behold the Great Redeemer Die," *Hymns* #191
> "In Humility, Our Savior," *Hymns* #172
> "Our Savior's Love," *Hymns* #113

SUMMARY

Jesus Christ was chosen and foreordained to come to earth to atone for our sins and teach us how to return to our Heavenly Father. Jesus Christ was not just a good man, effective teacher, or inspiring leader, but the Redeemer of the world! As members of the Church, we believe that the Savior lived on this earth and died for our sins, and that He still lives! Our lives should reflect those beliefs. Our actions should testify to all that we know He is coming again soon.

Our understanding of the divine mission of Jesus Christ should compel us to action, to show greater love and kindness, and to share His gospel with others. The gospel isn't just good news; it's *great* news! We should live our lives so that there will be absolutely no question members of the Church are Christians. Feasting daily on the scriptures and prayering sincerely will fill us with hope, joy, and a powerful testimony. By following Jesus Christ, we can find joy in this life and in the next.

QUOTES

"I weep for joy when I contemplate the significance of it all. To be redeemed is to be atoned—received in the close embrace of God with an expression not only of His forgiveness, but of our oneness of heart and mind" (Russell M. Nelson, "The Atonement," *Ensign*, November 1996).

"The Redeemer loves you and will help you do the essential things that bring happiness now and forever" (Richard G. Scott, "Jesus Christ, Our Redeemer," *Ensign*, May 1997).

"Ever and always [the Atonement] offers amnesty from transgression and from death if we will but repent. . . . Repentance is the key with which we can unlock the prison from inside. . . . Agency is ours to use it" (Boyd K. Packer, "Atonement, Agency, Accountability," *Ensign*, May 1988).

"[The Lord's] Atonement is the most transcendent event that ever has or ever will occur, from Creation's dawn through all the ages of a never-ending eternity" (Bruce R. McConkie, "The Purifying Power of Gethsemane," *Ensign*, May 1985).

"The Savior's birth, ministry, atoning sacrifice, Resurrection, and promised coming all bear witness to His divinity" (Ezra Taft Benson, "Five Marks of the Divinity of Jesus Christ," *Ensign,* December 2001).

• •

GOSPEL ART

Isaiah Writes of Christ's Birth—(113 KIT, 22 GAB)
The Nativity—(201 KIT, 30 GAB)
Boy Jesus in the Temple—(205 KIT, 34 GAB)
John the Baptist Baptizing Jesus—(208 KIT, 35 GAB)
Jesus Raising Jairus's Daughter—(215 KIT, 41 GAB)
Triumphal Entry—(223 KIT, 50 GAB)
Jesus Praying in Gethsemane—(227 KIT, 56 GAB)
The Betrayal of Jesus—(228 KIT)
The Crucifixion—(230 KIT, 57 GAB)
Burial of Jesus—(232 KIT, 58 GAB)
Mary and the Resurrected Lord—(233 KIT, 59 GAB)
Jesus Shows His Wounds—(234 KIT, 60 GAB)
The Ascension of Jesus—(236 KIT, 62 GAB)
Jesus at the Door—(237 KIT, 65 GAB)
The Second Coming—(238 KIT, 66 GAB)
The Resurrected Jesus Christ—(239 KIT)
The Empty Tomb—(245 KIT)

Jesus Teaching in the Western Hemisphere—(315 KIT, 82 GAB)

• •

VIDEOS

- ❧ "Jesus Christ Suffered for Us": https://goo.gl/rFB4Vr
- ❧ "He is Not Here, for He is Risen": https://goo.gl/eAwZHC
- ❧ "The Mediator": https://goo.gl/Wrb72E
- ❧ "To This End Was I Born": http://goo.gl/S6ycm3
- ❧ "Lifting Burdens: The Atonement of Jesus Christ": http://goo.gl/8y7QCu

• •

OBJECT LESSONS

- ❧ Show the class some different kinds of keys: old-fashioned keys, car keys, hotel card keys. Explain how the keys let you into appealing locations: fancy hotel rooms, luxury vehicles, bank safes, and so on. Some people judge their lives by the keys they possess. An education can be the key to a good career. A car can be a key to freedom. A good job can be the key to power and wealth. A key to a large home can represent success and security. There is only one key that opens the most important destination of all. Jesus Christ is the key to eternal life with Father in Heaven!

- ❧ Ask someone to draw a picture of a horse, a temple, or something complicated. Now give her a pattern to trace to draw the same thing. Jesus is our pattern to show us how to create our lives here on earth so that we can live an eternal life with Father in Heaven.

- ❧ Invite a volunteer to build a structure with building blocks on her lap. Ask the sisters sitting next to her to jiggle her shoulders or legs. Her structure will most likely fall. Now ask her to build one on top of a table at the front of the room. Invite some sisters to try to jiggle her again. This time, her structure won't fall because it has the stability of the table. Our testimonies need to be built on the Atonement of the Savior. That is the solid foundation that will prevent our testimonies and lives from falling apart.

- ❧ See more ideas in Lesson One.

• •

Church Magazine Articles

- M. Russell Ballard, "The Atonement and the Value of One Soul," *Ensign*, May 2004.
- Cecil O. Samuelson Jr., "What Does the Atonement Mean to You?" *Ensign*, April 2009.
- Marion G. Romney, "Christ's Atonement: The Gift Supreme," *Ensign*, December 1973.
- James E. Faust, "The Atonement: Our Greatest Hope," *Ensign*, November 2001.

Challenge

Write your testimony of the Savior and how you feel about the Atonement. Share it with your family, with someone serving a full-time mission, or with a nonmember.

Seminary Scripture Mastery

Helaman 5:12	Genesis 1:26–27
Isaiah 53:3–5	Matthew 16:15–19
Luke 24:36–39	John 3:5
John 17:3	1 Corinthians 15:20–22
D&C 19:16–19	D&C 76:22–24
D&C 130:22–23	

Preach My Gospel

Pages 34, 36–37, 48, 51–52, 60–61, 90, 105, 116–26

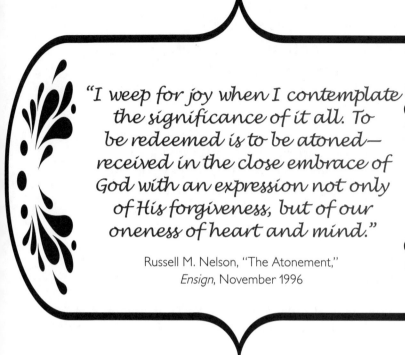

"I weep for joy when I contemplate the significance of it all. To be redeemed is to be atoned—received in the close embrace of God with an expression not only of His forgiveness, but of our oneness of heart and mind."

Russell M. Nelson, "The Atonement,"
Ensign, November 1996

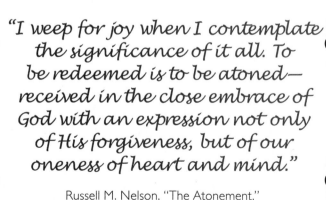

"I weep for joy when I contemplate the significance of it all. To be redeemed is to be atoned—received in the close embrace of God with an expression not only of His forgiveness, but of our oneness of heart and mind."

Russell M. Nelson, "The Atonement,"
Ensign, November 1996

Lesson Seven
Continuous Revelation
through Living Prophets

- -

MUSIC

"Come, Listen to a Prophet's Voice," *Hymns #21*
"Come, Sing to the Lord," *Hymns #10*
"God Bless Our Prophet Dear," *Hymns #24*
"Praise to the Man," *Hymns #27*
"We Thank Thee, O God, for a Prophet," *Hymns #19*

- -

SUMMARY

God communicates to His people through a living prophet, a man called through priesthood authority to represent Him. The prophet is also the President of The Church of Jesus Christ of Latter-day Saints and holds the keys of the kingdom on earth. The prophet receives revelation for the Church and leads the administration of priesthood ordinances. He is also called a seer and revelator. By following the Lord's chosen mouthpiece, we will never be led astray.

When we sustain the prophet by the show of our raised hand in church, we are not voting for him; we are affirming our support and commitment to follow the Lord's anointed mouthpiece on earth.

- -

QUOTES

"A prophet . . . is the authorized representative of the Lord. While the world may not recognize him, the important requirement is that God speaks through him" (A. Theodore Tuttle, "What Is a Living Prophet?" *Ensign*, July 1973).

"Sustaining support of prophets, seers, and revelators is not in the upraised hand alone, but more so in our courage, testimony, and faith to listen to, heed, and follow them" (Dennis B. Neuenschwander, "Living Prophets, Seers, and Revelators," *Ensign*, November 2000).

"When we sustain, it means we *do* something about our belief. Our testimony of the prophet turns into action when we sustain him" (Janette Hales Beckham, "Sustaining the Living Prophets," *Ensign*, May 1996).

"Surely one of the crowning blessings of membership in this Church is the blessing of being led by living prophets of God" (Kevin R. Duncan, "Our Very Survival," *Ensign*, November 2010).

"Prophets often raise a voice of warning but also provide steady, pragmatic counsel to help us weather the storms of life" (Steven E. Snow, "Get On with Our Lives," *Ensign*, May 2009).

• •

GOSPEL ART

Building the Ark—(102 KIT, 7 GAB)
Noah and the Ark with Animals—(103 KIT, 8 GAB)
Abraham Taking Isaac to be Sacrificed—(105 KIT, 9 GAB)
Moses and the Burning Bush—(107 KIT, 13 GAB)
Boy Samuel Called by the Lord—(111 KIT, 18 GAB)
Enoch and His People Are Taken up to God—(120 KIT, 16 GAB)
Lehi Prophesying to the People of Jerusalem—(300 KIT, 67 GAB)
Nephi Subdues His Rebellious Brothers—(303 KIT)
Enos Praying—(305 KIT, 70 GAB)
Mormon Abridging the Plates—(306 KIT, 73 GAB)
King Benjamin Addresses His People—(307 KIT, 74 GAB)
Abinadi before King Noah—(308 KIT, 75 GAB)
Samuel the Lamanite on the Wall—(314 KIT, 81 GAB)
Mormon Bids Farewell to a Once Great Nation—(319 KIT)
The Prophet Joseph Smith—(401 KIT, 122 GAB)
Latter-day Prophets—(506–22 KIT, 122–37 GAB)
Brigham Young—(507 KIT)
John Taylor—(508 KIT)
Wilford Woodruff—(509 KIT)
Lorenzo Snow—(510 KIT)
Joseph F. Smith—(511 KIT)
Heber J. Grant—(512 KIT)
George Albert Smith—(513 KIT)
David O. McKay—(514 KIT)

Joseph Fielding Smith—(515 KIT)
Harold B. Lee—(516 KIT)
Spencer W. Kimball—(517 KIT)
Ezra Taft Benson—(518 KIT)
Howard W. Hunter—(519 KIT)
Gordon B. Hinckley—(520 KIT)
Sustaining Our Leaders—(610 KIT)

• •

VIDEOS

- ❧ "Follow the Prophet": https://goo.gl/dXuEdz
- ❧ "Life's Greatest Decisions": https://goo.gl/UrzAkz
- ❧ "We Need Living Prophets": https://goo.gl/fz8bXk
- ❧ "A Steady, Reassuring Voice": https://goo.gl/K7HLhR

• •

OBJECT LESSONS

- ❧ Tell the class that a coin represents ancient and modern prophets. Ask them which side of the coin is more important. Then ask if the two sides of the coin can be separated. Explain that both sides of the coin work together for the same purpose, just as all prophets throughout the ages have had the common goal of bringing people to Jesus Christ.
- ❧ Invite the sisters to sign a birthday card for the prophet. You can find out his birthday on LDS.org.
- ❧ Gift-wrap two boxes. Leave one empty and put some treats in the other one. Tell the class that one of the boxes has something special in it, while the other one has nothing. Ask a volunteer to choose a box. Let the volunteer see what's inside the box and ask the class if they want her to decide for them which box they'll get. Of course they'll say yes, because she now knows what's in both boxes. We follow the prophet because he has seen what's in the box of life! He knows what choices we need to make in order to receive eternal rewards.
- ❧ Hold a peanut with the shell in your hand behind your back and tell the class that you're holding something that has never been seen by human eyes before. Of course, they won't believe you. Ask

46

for some volunteers to take a peek and tell the class if what you're saying is true or not. When they testify that you're telling the truth, ask how many believe now that there are witnesses. Some still won't. (They must be nuts.) Talk about how the prophets have seen and testify of truth. Some in the world will refuse to believe them. Will you?

Church Magazine Articles

- F. Michael Watson, "His Servants, the Prophets," *Ensign*, May 2009.
- David B. Haight, "A Prophet Chosen of the Lord," *Ensign*, May 1986.
- Jeffrey R. Holland, " 'My Words . . . Never Cease,' " *Ensign*, May 2008.
- Jeffrey R. Holland, "Prophets in the Land Again," *Ensign*, November 2006.
- Dieter F. Uchtdorf, "Heeding the Voice of the Prophets," *Ensign*, July 2008.
- Gordon B. Hinckley, "We Thank Thee, O God, for a Prophet," *Ensign*, September 1991.

Challenge

Read talks from the most recent general conference to hear what our current prophet and apostles counseled us to do. Make a list of the things you need to work on in your life in order to follow the prophet 100 percent.

Seminary Scripture Mastery

1 Nephi 3:7	Abraham 3:22–23
Matthew 16:15–19	Ephesians 4:11–14

PREACH MY GOSPEL

Pages 6–7, 32, 35–36, 44–45, 66, 75, 88

• •

"Human judgment and logical thinking will not be enough to get answers to the questions that matter most in life. We need revelation from God."

Henry B. Eyring, "Continuing Revelation," *Ensign*, November 2014

"Human judgment and logical thinking will not be enough to get answers to the questions that matter most in life. We need revelation from God."

Henry B. Eyring, "Continuing Revelation," *Ensign*, November 2014

"Human judgment and logical thinking will not be enough to get answers to the questions that matter most in life. We need revelation from God."

Henry B. Eyring, "Continuing Revelation," *Ensign*, November 2014

"Human judgment and logical thinking will not be enough to get answers to the questions that matter most in life. We need revelation from God."

Henry B. Eyring, "Continuing Revelation," *Ensign*, November 2014

Lesson Eight
Taking the Gospel to All the World

. . . .

MUSIC

"Called to Serve," *Hymns #249*
"How Will They Know?" *Children's Songbook #182*
"I Hope They Call Me on a Mission," *Children's Songbook #169*
"I Want to Be a Missionary Now," *Children's Songbook #168*
"We'll Bring the World His Truth (Army of Helaman),"
Children's Songbook #172

. . . .

SUMMARY

There are many people in the world who are pure in heart, who would embrace the fulness of the gospel if they were given the opportunity. We have been given the knowledge of saving ordinances, as well as the divinely commissioned call to provide them to the nations of the earth.

When we truly feel the Savior's love, we have the natural desire to extend it to those around us. When we do, our joy will be felt for eternity. The Lord entrusts us with this important work, and it is our privilege to bring light to a dark world. Our righteous examples can illuminate our neighborhoods and draw the pure in heart to us.

When we help prepare young men and women to serve full-time missions and support them with prayers, food, finances, and referrals while they are laboring in the field, the Lord is pleased with our missionary efforts. We will have an even greater desire to open our mouths and share what we know with a world that is seeking truth and direction. What a thrill it is to be a part of the exciting wave of missionary work happening right now as the Lord hastens His work!

In the spirit of love and kindness, our missionary work is about inviting people, not convincing them, to learn more. Rather than debate doctrine with nonbelievers, we gently love them and show them the Savior's love. The most important part of effective missionary work is not our carefully chosen words, but the spirit with which we teach. This is the Lord's work and one of the most important things we can do here on earth.

• •

QUOTES

" 'This isn't missionary work. This is missionary fun' " (Neil L. Andersen, "It's a Miracle," *Ensign*, May 2013).

"We must develop love for people. Our hearts must go out to them in the pure love of the gospel, in a desire to lift them, to build them up, to point them to a higher, finer life that eventually will lead to exaltation in the celestial kingdom of God" (Ezra Taft Benson, "Keys to Successful Member-Missionary Work," *Ensign*, September 1990).

"The First Presidency has said that one of the threefold missions of the Church is to proclaim the gospel. If we accept this mission, we should be willing to center our efforts on bringing souls unto the Lord on condition of repentance. . . . In talking of faith and saving souls, you should understand that when the Spirit is present, people are not offended when you share your feelings about the gospel" (M. Russell Ballard, "We Proclaim the Gospel," *Ensign*, November 1986).

"For the Savior's mandate to share the gospel to become part of who we are, we need to make member missionary work a way of life" (Quentin L. Cook, "Be a Missionary All Your Life," *Ensign*, September 2008).

"It is impractical for us to expect that (full-time) missionaries alone can warn the millions in the world. Members must be finders. . . . If we are in tune, the Spirit of the Lord will speak to us and guide us to those with whom we should share the gospel. The Lord will help us if we will but listen" (Ezra Taft Benson, "President Kimball's Vision of Missionary Work," *Ensign*, July 1985).

"When we received the special blessing of knowledge of the gospel of Jesus Christ and took upon ourselves the name of Christ by entering the waters of baptism, we also accepted the obligation to share the gospel with others" (L. Tom Perry, "The Past Way of Facing the Future," *Ensign*, November 2009).

51

"The standard of truth has been erected: no unhallowed hand can stop the work from progressing, persecution may rage, mobs may combine, armies may assemble, calumny may defame, but the truth of God will go forth boldly, nobly, and independent till it has penetrated every continent, visited every clime, swept every country, and sounded in every ear, till the purposes of God shall be accomplished and the great Jehovah shall say the work is done" (Joseph Smith, *History of the Church, Times & Seasons*, 1 March 1842, 709).

"After all that has been said, the greatest and most important duty is to preach the Gospel" (Joseph Smith, *History of the Church*, 2:478).

"Missionary work is not just one of the 88 keys on a piano that is occasionally played; it is a major chord in a compelling melody that needs to be played continuously throughout our lives if we are to remain in harmony with our commitment to the gospel of Jesus Christ" (Quentin L. Cook, "Be a Missionary All Your Life," *Ensign*, September 2008).

Gospel Art

Daniel Refusing the King's Meat and Wine—(114 KIT, 23 GAB)
Esther—(21 GAB)
Boy Jesus in the Temple—(205 KIT, 34 GAB)
John Preaching in the Wilderness—(207 KIT)
Calling of the Fishermen—(209 KIT, 37 GAB)
Mary and Martha—(219 KIT, 45 GAB)
Go Ye Therefore—(235 KIT, 61 GAB)
Abinadi before King Noah—(308 KIT, 75 GAB)
Alma Baptizes in the Waters of Mormon—(309 KIT, 76 GAB)
Ammon Defends the Flocks of King Lamoni—(310 KIT, 78 GAB)
Four Missionaries to the Lamanites—(418 KIT)
Missionaries Teach the Gospel of Jesus Christ—(612 KIT)
Missionaries: Elders—(109 GAB)
Missionaries: Sisters—(110 GAB)

Videos

⚹ "Missionary work": https://goo.gl/18RTEp

- "The Church to Fill the Earth": https://goo.gl/o7MUc0
- "Developing the Faith to Find": https://goo.gl/G9OiZv
- "Loving and Serving Others": https://goo.gl/lquDA1
- "The Opportunity of a Lifetime": https://goo.gl/BD6mqx
- "Why Mormons Send Missionaries around the World": https://goo.gl/DNxUx3

- -

OBJECT LESSONS

- Invite the sisters to be creative in pairs and take turns doing "door approaches" by knocking on the door to your classroom and presenting a gospel message. You'll be amazed at how innovative they'll be!

- Set up a row of dominoes on the front table and then watch the chain reaction as you knock the first one down. Compare that to all of the lives that are touched for good by just one member of the Church being a good missionary.

- Display a large basket of goodies on the table at the front of the class and begin to eat from it, expressing great delight. Ask the class to share why they love the gospel so much. Continue snacking and then explain that when we enjoy the blessings of the gospel without sharing it with others, it's like you're having a basket of goodies you love and not sharing it with the class! Pass the basket around and invite everyone to join you in eating yummy treats. At the end of the lesson, ask the sisters how many of them didn't take a treat, ate it right away, or planned on saving it for later. Explain that doing missionary work is similar. Even when we share the sweet gospel with others, some people will accept and embrace it right away, some won't accept it at all, and others might accept it but not for many years.

- Invite the full-time missionaries to share some conversion stories and experiences with your class.

- Before class, put a bunch of candy in a bag. Tell the class that we often feel we can't make any difference as just one person. Show one piece of candy and explain that it represents you, a member of the Church. Show another piece of candy, which represents one person you talk to about the gospel. That person then tells someone else about the gospel who tells another person, and so on. Add a piece of candy next to each person who talks about the gospel. Talk about how our simple efforts can grow the Church exponentially. Pass around the candy to the class, illustrating that sharing the gospel can be *sweet*.

❧ Place a rock in a bowl and explain that it represents the hearts of some people. Use a squirt gun to spray some water on the rock to illustrate how when we try to explain the gospel to hard-hearted people it just rolls off. Show a sponge in the shape of a heart. Use the squirt gun to spray some water on it and point out how the sponge quickly absorbs the water. Some people will soak up the gospel like sponges. Jesus Christ is the Living Water. Not everyone will be ready to accept the gospel, but we still can offer them the opportunity.

CHURCH MAGAZINE ARTICLES

❧ Earl C. Tingey, "Missionary Service," *Ensign,* May 1998.
❧ Thomas S. Monson, "That All May Hear," *Ensign*, May 1995.
❧ M. Russell Ballard, "Creating a Gospel-Sharing Home," *Ensign*, May 2006.
❧ Dallin H. Oaks, "Sharing the Gospel," *Ensign*, November 2001.
❧ Dallin H Oaks, "The Role of Members in Conversion," *Ensign*, March 2003.
❧ Ezra Taft Benson, "President Kimball's Vision of Missionary Work," *Ensign*, July 1985.

CHALLENGE

Invite the full-time missionaries in your area over to dinner. Ask them about their investigators and find out what you can do to help. Invite them to teach one of their investigators in your home or go with them to teach.

SEMINARY SCRIPTURE MASTERY

Moroni 10:4–5   Isaiah 29:13–14

D&C 18:10–11   Joseph Smith—History 1:15–20
D&C 18:15–16

• •

PREACH MY GOSPEL

Pages 1–2, 4–6, 8–13, 19–21, 105, 107–09, 127, 155–58, 175–76, 182–88, 190–91, 195–99, 203

• •

"We must develop love for people. Our hearts must go out to them in the pure love of the gospel, in a desire to lift them, to build them up, to point them to a higher, finer life that eventually will lead to exaltation in the celestial kingdom of God."

Ezra Taft Benson, "Keys to Successful Member-Missionary Work," *Ensign*, September 1990

"We must develop love for people. Our hearts must go out to them in the pure love of the gospel, in a desire to lift them, to build them up, to point them to a higher, finer life that eventually will lead to exaltation in the celestial kingdom of God."

Ezra Taft Benson, "Keys to Successful Member-Missionary Work," *Ensign*, September 1990

"We must develop love for people. Our hearts must go out to them in the pure love of the gospel, in a desire to lift them, to build them up, to point them to a higher, finer life that eventually will lead to exaltation in the celestial kingdom of God."

Ezra Taft Benson, "Keys to Successful Member-Missionary Work," *Ensign*, September 1990

Lesson Nine
The Law of Tithing

MUSIC

"Because I Have Been Given Much," *Hymns* #219
"We Give Thee But Thine Own," *Hymns* #218
"I'm Glad to Pay a Tithing," *Children's Songbook* #150
"I Want to Give the Lord My Tenth," *Children's Songbook* #150

• •

SUMMARY

Everything we have is a gift from God. Paying an honest tithe is a way to show gratitude to Him and help build His kingdom here on earth. Tithing on our increase is a test of our obedience and our willingness to put aside the things of mortality for loftier, more spiritual pursuits. It doesn't take money to pay tithing; it takes faith! We can tithe our time, in addition to money, as we live the principle of sacrifice.

As with all commandments, we are blessed when we have an attitude of obedience. Tithing supports the many wonderful programs and facilities the Church offers to us and our families. You can do more with 90 percent of your money and the Lord's help than you can with 100 percent on your own.

• •

QUOTES

"Some people say, 'I can't afford to pay tithing.' Those who place their faith in the Lord's promises say, 'I can't afford not to pay tithing.' . . . In a general conference in 1912, Elder Heber J. Grant declared: 'I bear witness—and I know that the witness I bear is true—that the men and the women who have been absolutely honest with God, who have paid their tithing, . . . God has given them wisdom whereby they have been able to utilize the remaining nine-tenths, and it has been of greater value to them, and they have accomplished more with it than they would if they had not been honest with the Lord,'" (Dallin H. Oaks, "Tithing," *Ensign*, May 1994).

"The Lord has established the law of tithing as the law of revenue of His Church. . . . It is also a law by which we show our loyalty to the Lord" (Earl C. Tingey, "The Law of Tithing," *Ensign*, May 2002).

"Tithing is a principle that is fundamental to the personal happiness and well-being of the Church members worldwide, both rich and poor" (James E. Faust, "Opening the Windows of Heaven," *Ensign*, November 1998).

"We should pay [tithes and offerings] as a personal expression of love to a generous and merciful Father in Heaven" (Jeffrey R. Holland, "Like a Watered Garden," *Ensign,* November 2001).

Gospel Art

Adam and Eve Kneeling at an Altar—(4 GAB)
Abraham Taking Isaac to be Sacrificed—(9 GAB)
The Ten Commandments—(14 GAB)
Joseph and Mary Travel to Bethlehem—(29 GAB)
The Ten Lepers—(46 GAB)
Christ and the Rich Young Ruler—(48 GAB)
Jesus Cleansing the Temple—(51 GAB)
Payment of Tithing—(113 GAB)
A Tithe is a Tenth Part—(114 GAB)

Videos

❧ "Tithing": https://goo.gl/EEnz9g
❧ "The Lord's Richest Blessings": https://goo.gl/Zvr5i0
❧ "The Widow's Mites": https://goo.gl/835qf6

Object Lessons

❧ Give some Legos to a sister and ask her to build a house with a window. Before she gets too far, ask her to give you 10 percent back. When she does, give her even more Legos. Keep doing that as she tries to build her house. Explain that when we make a small sacrifice, the Lord blesses us even more abundantly, sometimes with physical blessings but always with spiritual ones! Talk about what "the windows of heaven" means that will open with blessings when we tithe.

꙾ Give a volunteer ten pieces of small candy. Ask her to give you one back before she eats any of them. It should be easy for her to do since you just gave her ten. In contrast, give another volunteer ten pieces of candy and allow her to eat nine of them before you ask for her last piece of candy. (It's supposed to be harder to resist eating the last one.) Talk about how it's easier to tithe if we give back before we are down to our last funds.

꙾ Have the sisters color and cut out pictures that can be used in a family home evening lesson about tithing. Talk about how paying tithing isn't just putting money in an envelope, but rather, it's helping real people.

Church Magazine Articles

꙾ Jeffrey R. Holland, "Like a Watered Garden," *Ensign,* November 2001.

꙾ Earl C. Tingey, "The Law of Tithing," *Ensign*, May 2002.

꙾ Robert D. Hales, "Tithing: A Test of Faith with Eternal Blessings," *Ensign*, November 2002.

꙾ Dallin H. Oaks, "Tithing," *Ensign*, May 1994.

Challenge

Schedule an appointment with your bishop to do tithing settlement this year. They're usually scheduled in November and December. Bring the bishopric some treats to help them get through the long hours they serve on those tithing settlement days!

Seminary Scripture Mastery

1 Nephi 3:7	Mosiah 4:30
Alma 37:35	Exodus 20:3–17
Isaiah 29:13–14	Malachi 3:8–10

John 14:15   D&C 58:27
D&C 82:10

• •

PREACH MY GOSPEL

Pages 72, 75, 78–79, 122

• •

"Some people say, 'I can't afford to pay tithing.' Those who place their faith in the Lord's promises say, 'I can't afford not to pay tithing.'"

Dallin H. Oaks, "Tithing,"
Ensign, May 1994

"Some people say, 'I can't afford to pay tithing.' Those who place their faith in the Lord's promises say, 'I can't afford not to pay tithing.'"

Dallin H. Oaks, "Tithing,"
Ensign, May 1994

Lesson Ten
The Scriptures—The Most Profitable of All Study

MUSIC

"As I Search the Holy Scriptures," *Hymns* #277
"Book of Mormon Stories," *Children's Songbook* #118
"From Homes of Saints Glad Songs Arise," *Hymns* #297
"The Books in the Book of Mormon," *Children's Songbook* #119
"Search, Ponder, and Pray," *Children's Songbook* #109

SUMMARY

An earnest desire for truth can create a powerful experience when searching the sacred pages of scripture. The Lord has preserved in holy writ the information He knows will help us in mortality and lead us to Him. We can find more comfort and wisdom in the scriptures than in all other books ever written.

As members of the Church, we are so blessed to have additional clarifying scriptures in the Book of Mormon, Doctrine and Covenants, and Pearl of Great Price. The words in the scriptures come from a loving Heavenly Father, who wants us to know what is required to again enter into His presence. As parents, it is vital to our children's salvation that we not only introduce them to the scriptures but show them how to search the scriptures, understand them, ascertain their truthfulness, and apply the teachings to their lives. All scriptures testify of Jesus Christ and are designed to bring us closer to Him. The words from living prophets are also considered scripture.

QUOTES

"Don't yield to Satan's lie that you don't have time to study the scriptures. Choose to take time to study them. Feasting on the word of God each day is more important than sleep, school, work, television shows, video games, or social media. You may need to reorganize your priorities to provide time for the study of the word of God. If so, do it!" (Richard G. Scott, "Make the Exercise of Faith Your First Priority," *Ensign*, November 2014).

"Through reading the scriptures, we can gain the assurance of the Spirit that that which we read has come of God for the enlightenment, blessing, and joy of his children" (Gordon B. Hinckley, "Feasting upon the Scriptures," *Ensign*, December 1985).

"The holy scriptures are like letters from home telling us how we can draw near to our Father in Heaven" (Ardeth G. Kapp, "The Holy Scriptures: Letters from Home," *Ensign*, November 1985).

"If you have not already developed the habit of daily scripture study, start now and keep studying in order to be prepared for your responsibilities in this life and in the eternities" (Julie B. Beck, "My Soul Delighteth in the Scriptures," *Ensign*, May 2004).

"As a person studies the words of the Lord and obeys them, he or she draws closer to the Savior and obtains a greater desire to live a righteous life" (Merrill J. Bateman, "Coming unto Christ by Searching the Scriptures," *Ensign*, November 1992).

GOSPEL ART

Isaiah Writes of Christ's Birth—(113 KIT, 22 GAB)
Boy Jesus in the Temple—(205 KIT, 34 GAB)
Mormon Abridging the Plates—(306 KIT, 73 GAB)
Moroni Hides the Plates in the Hill Cumorah—(320 KIT, 86 GAB)
Christ Asks for the Records—(323 KIT)
The Gold Plates—(325 KIT)
The Bible and Book of Mormon: Two Witnesses—(326 KIT)
Joseph Smith Seeks Wisdom in the Bible—(402 KIT, 89 GAB)
Saving the Book of Commandments—(409 KIT)
Translating the Book of Mormon—(416 KIT, 92 GAB)
Search the Scriptures—(617 KIT)

VIDEOS

❧ "Study the Scriptures": https://goo.gl/HLdxx4
❧ "The Maze": https://goo.gl/qCiJLf

❧ "King James Bible Anniversary": https://goo.gl/H79bAA
❧ "Scriptures—More Precious Than Gold and Sweeter Than Honey": https://goo.gl/XLq1kB

· ·

OBJECT LESSONS

❧ Hold up a lollipop or some other piece of candy that has a wrapper. Ask for a volunteer who likes candy. Invite the volunteer to put the candy in her mouth. When she starts to take off the wrapper, say, "I didn't say you could take the wrapper off. I just said you could put it in your mouth." Have her put the candy in her mouth with the wrapper on and ask her how it tastes. Ask her how long she thinks it will take for her saliva to dissolve the wrapper before she can taste the candy. Point out that her saliva has the ability to dissolve the hard candy, but not the wrapper. Talk about how the scriptures are like the candy. Because the scriptures were written by the power of the Holy Ghost, they can't be understood unless a person has the help of the Holy Ghost. The mind of man alone does not have the ability to "take off the wrapper." President Howard W. Hunter said, "There is nothing more helpful than prayer to open our understanding of the scriptures" ("Reading the Scriptures," *Ensign*, November 1979). Finally, invite the volunteer and the whole class to enjoy some candy (without the wrappers on) during the rest of the lesson.

❧ Bring a plate of cookies and ask for volunteers to demonstrate different styles of eating: abstain, sample, snack, gorge, nibble, eat, and feast. Now compare those styles to how we study the scriptures, reminding the class that we should feast upon the words of Christ.

❧ Show the class two pictures that seem alike but have a few differences. Have the class point out the differences. In order to align our life with the Lord's will, we need to follow His example found in the scriptures and change our life to match His model for us.

❧ Ask a class member to play a hymn on the harmonica. (Pick someone who doesn't know how to play it.) When they explain that they can't do it, ask them how they could learn. The answer is to study a manual or learn from someone who can. The same applies to learning to be like Heavenly Father; we can learn about Him in the scriptures and we can follow the Savior, who is like Him. Daily practice makes perfect!

ꙮ Listen to part of the podcast "Chapter 10: Scriptures" at http://goo.gl/rkesor. The sisters can mark seminary scripture mastery verses in their scriptures while they listen.

• •

CHURCH MAGAZINE ARTICLES

ꙮ "Feasting on the Word," *Ensign,* March 2003.

ꙮ Henry B. Eyring, "A Discussion on Scripture Study," *Ensign,* July 2005.

ꙮ Ardeth G. Kapp, "The Holy Scriptures: Letters from Home," *Ensign,* November 1985.

ꙮ Dallin H. Oaks, "Scripture Reading and Revelation," *Ensign,* January 1995.

ꙮ Julie B. Beck, "My Soul Delighteth in the Scriptures," *Ensign,* May 2004.

ꙮ M. Russell Ballard, "The Miracle of the Holy Bible," *Ensign,* May 2007.

ꙮ L. Tom Perry, "Give Heed unto the Word of the Lord," *Ensign,* 2000.

ꙮ Lenet H. Read, "How the Bible Came to Be" Series, *Ensign,* January–September 1982.

• •

CHALLENGE

Mark all of the seminary scripture mastery verses in your scriptures. Begin memorizing them with your family. Have an old-fashioned scripture chase! That's a game seminary students have played for many years. The teacher gives clues, and the students race to see who can find the correct scripture the fastest.

• •

SEMINARY SCRIPTURE MASTERY

2 Nephi 9:28–29	2 Nephi 32:3
Ezekiel 37:15–17	Amos 3:7

2 Timothy 3:15–17   Joseph Smith—History 1:15–20

• •

PREACH MY GOSPEL

Pages 17, 19, 22–24, 38, 103–14, 180–81.

• •

"Don't yield to Satan's lie that you don't have time to study the scriptures. Choose to take time to study them. Feasting on the word of God each day is more important than sleep, school, work, television shows, video games, or social media. You may need to reorganize your priorities to provide time for the study of the word of God. If so, do it!"

Richard G. Scott, "Make the Exercise of Faith Your First Priority," *Ensign*, November 2014

"Don't yield to Satan's lie that you don't have time to study the scriptures. Choose to take time to study them. Feasting on the word of God each day is more important than sleep, school, work, television shows, video games, or social media. You may need to reorganize your priorities to provide time for the study of the word of God. If so, do it!"

Richard G. Scott, "Make the Exercise of Faith Your First Priority," *Ensign*, November 2014

Lesson Eleven
True Greatness

. . . .

MUSIC

"I Want to Live the Gospel," *Children's Songbook* #148
"Keep the Commandments," *Hymns* #303
"Sweet Is the Peace the Gospel Brings," *Hymns* #14
"Lead Me into Life Eternal," *Hymns* #45
"With All the Power of Heart and Tongue," *Hymns* #79

. . . .

SUMMARY

The world defines greatness in terms of a successful career, fortune, and fame, but the Lord recognizes the strength and courage of living the gospel on a daily basis as being truly great. Continuously striving to be obedient and true to our covenants amidst everyday challenges leads to true greatness.

Serving others, building faith, and loving one another don't often make headline news or win us awards, but the Lord is more concerned with the small, consistent acts that make us more Christlike each day. Because the applause of the world only brings temporary satisfaction, we need to focus our energy on what will bring eternal joy.

. . . .

QUOTES

"That man is greatest and most blessed and joyful whose life most closely approaches the pattern of the Christ. This has nothing to do with earthly wealth, power, or prestige. The only true test of greatness, blessedness, joyfulness is how close a life can come to being like the Master, Jesus Christ. He is the right way, the full truth, and the abundant life" (Ezra Taft Benson, "Jesus Christ—Gifts and Expectations," *Ensign*, December 1988).

"I am confident that there are many great, unnoticed, and forgotten heroes among us. I am speaking of those of you who quietly and consistently do the things you ought to do" (Howard W. Hunter, "What Is True Greatness?" *Ensign*, September 1987).

"The man who so walks in the light and wisdom and power of God, will at the last, by the very force of association, make the light and wisdom and power of God his own—weaving those bright rays into a chain divine, linking himself forever to God and God to him" (B. H. Roberts, "Brigham Young: A Character Sketch," *Improvement Era*, June 1903, 574).

Gospel Art

Jesus Christ—(240 KIT, 1 GAB)
Adam and Eve Kneeling at an Altar—(4 GAB)
Adam and Eve Teaching Their Children—(5 GAB)
City of Zion Is Taken Up—(6 GAB)
The Ten Commandments—(14 GAB)
Ruth Gleaning in the Fields—(17 GAB)
Daniel Refusing the King's Meat and Wine—(114 KIT, 23 GAB)
Three Men in the Fiery Furnace—(116 KIT, 25 GAB)
Daniel in the Lions' Den—(117 KIT, 26 GAB)
Parable of the Ten Virgins—(53 GAB)
The Liahona—(302 KIT, 68 GAB)
Enos Praying—(305 KIT, 72 GAB)
King Benjamin Addresses His People—(307 KIT, 74 GAB)
Alma Baptizes in the Waters of Mormon—(309 KIT, 76 GAB)
Family Prayer—(606 KIT, 112 GAB)
Payment of tithing—(113 GAB)

Videos

- "Living the Gospel": https://goo.gl/5vFAk8
- "Living the Gospel Brings Power": https://goo.gl/SbUZwY
- "I'm a Mormon, 2014": https://goo.gl/38kwjT
- "Living the Gospel Joyful": https://goo.gl/4hP9yH

OBJECT LESSONS

❧ Divide the class into three teams to write all of the simple ways we can live the gospel every day, starting with the letter A and going to Z. When you say go, each team sends a sister up to the front of the room to write on the chalkboard, starting with letter A, and then goes back to her group. Another sister from her group runs up to the chalkboard to write something else that starts with the letter B. No team can write the same thing as another team. The team that can get to letter Z first wins.

❧ Type up the questions in the "Suggestions for Study and Teaching" section in the manual and cut them into strips of paper that the sisters can pull out of a bag to answer. Also include strips of paper that say, "You get a treat from the prize bag!" so that every now and then a sister will be surprised. Prizes can include pieces of candy, bookmarks, or whatever you can come up with.

❧ Pass out pieces of cardstock that have been cut to look like bookmarks. Invite the sisters to color and design their bookmarks during the lesson. Encourage them to include a quote or image that will remind them of the joy they feel when they live the gospel valiantly each day.

CHURCH MAGAZINE ARTICLES

❧ D. Todd Christofferson, "Reflections on a Consecrated Life," *Ensign*, November 2010.

❧ Quentin L. Cook, "The True Path to Happiness," *Ensign*, June 2011.

❧ Daniel Miller, "One Minute to Greatness," *New Era*, October 1980.

❧ "Living the Gospel Blesses My Family," *Friend*, September 2014.

CHALLENGE

Write a list of all the things you should be doing to live the gospel completely. You might feel overwhelmed by seeing such a long list, but don't allow yourself to feel guilty or hopeless. Simply pick one thing on that list and create a plan to do that one thing better every day for one month. Once you have incorporated that gospel principle into your life, choose another one from the list and begin to work on that. Take it one day at a time.

• •

SEMINARY SCRIPTURE MASTERY

1 Nephi 3:7	2 Nephi 32:8–9
Mosiah 3:19	Mosiah 4:30
Alma 37:35	Moroni 7:45, 47–48
Exodus 20:3–17	Joshua 24:15
1 Samuel 16:7	Isaiah 29:13–14
Matthew 5:14–16	John 14:15
John 17:3	D&C 1:37–38
D&C 19:16–19	D&C 58:27
D&C 64:9–11	D&C 82:10
D&C 130:18–19	

• •

PREACH MY GOSPEL

Pages 3, 5, 8, 19, 66, 72, 75–76, 88, 89, 115, 122–26, 168–69, 221

• •

"THE ONLY TRUE TEST OF GREATNESS,
BLESSEDNESS, JOYFULNESS IS HOW CLOSE a
LIFE CAN COME TO BEING LIKE THE Master,
Jesus Christ. He IS THE RIGHT WAY, THE
FULL TRUTH, and THE ABUNDANT LIFE."

Ezra Taft Benson, "Jesus Christ—Gifts and
Expectations," *Ensign*, December 1988

"THE ONLY TRUE TEST OF GREATNESS,
BLESSEDNESS, JOYFULNESS IS HOW CLOSE a
LIFE CAN COME TO BEING LIKE THE Master,
Jesus Christ. He IS THE RIGHT WAY, THE
FULL TRUTH, and THE ABUNDANT LIFE."

Ezra Taft Benson, "Jesus Christ—Gifts and
Expectations," *Ensign*, December 1988

Lesson Twelve
Come Back and Feast at
the Table of the Lord

● ●

MUSIC

"Dear to the Heart of the Shepherd," *Hymns* #221
"The Lord Is My Shepherd," *Hymns* #108
"Come, All Whose Souls Are Lighted," *Hymns* #268
"Come, All Ye Saints of Zion," *Hymns* #38
"The Holy Ghost," *Children's Songbook* #105
"The Still Small Voice," *Children's Songbook* #106

● ●

SUMMARY

The parable of the lost sheep teaches us about the love of the Savior
for the one. It is a sacred duty and honor to help the Lord feed His
sheep and find those who are lost. With kindness and patience, we can
befriend those who are less active in the Church and help them feel
the joy they once felt when they first joined the Church.

With the companionship of the Holy Ghost, we can receive inspiration about what to say and how to invite less active members back
into the fold. The goal is to help them remember the sacred covenants
they made at baptism and gain a desire to participate in additional
ordinances that will bless their lives. The Holy Ghost has been given
to us by a loving Heavenly Father to provide comfort, guidance, and
a witness for truth.

● ●

QUOTES

"Come back to the serenity that distills from the decision to live
the commandments of your Elder Brother, Jesus the Christ. . . . Love
engenders faith in Christ's plan of happiness, provides courage to
begin the process of repentance, strengthens the resolve to be obedient to His teachings, and opens the door of service, welcoming in the

feelings of self-worth and of being loved and needed" (Richard G. Scott, "We Love You—Please Come Back," *Ensign*, May 1986).

"The simplicity of this ordinance may cause us to overlook its significance. These four words—'Receive the Holy Ghost'—are not a passive pronouncement; rather, they constitute a priesthood injunction—an authoritative admonition to act and not simply to be acted upon" (David A. Bednar, "Receive the Holy Ghost," *Ensign*, November 2010).

"We need the help of the Holy Ghost if we are to make our way safely through what the Apostle Paul called the 'perilous times' in which we now live" (Gerald N. Lund, "Opening Our Hearts," *Ensign*, May 2008).

"Testimony brings to us a knowledge that the gospel is true, but conversion by the Spirit brings something more" (Loren C. Dunn, "Fire and the Holy Ghost," *Ensign*, June 1995).

GOSPEL ART

Boy Samuel Called by the Lord—(111 KIT, 18 GAB)
The Liahona—(302 KIT, 68 GAB)
Abinadi before King Noah—(308 KIT, 75 GAB)
Samuel the Lamanite on the Wall—(314 KIT, 81 GAB)
The Gift of the Holy Ghost—(602 KIT, 105 GAB)
John the Baptist Baptizing Jesus—(208 KIT, 35 GAB)

VIDEOS

⁂ "Feed My Sheep": https://goo.gl/OxPr5f
⁂ "Jesus Declares the Parable of the Lost Sheep": https://goo.gl/6FZ9H9
⁂ "Ye Have Done It Unto Me": https://goo.gl/ldMyAb
⁂ "The Good Shepherd": https://goo.gl/Ga5Qfg
⁂ "Waiting for the Prodigal": https://goo.gl/el8bQI
⁂ "Feeling the Holy Ghost": https://goo.gl/KGBsmn

Object Lessons

❧ Have the class listen to the voices of apostles and prophets and try to guess whose voices they are. Then play some voices of members of their family. Talk about how it is much easier to recognize a voice when you are familiar with it. We need to develop relationships of trust with our less-active friends so that they can feel comfortable and safe returning to the Church. We can teach them how to recognize the still, small voice of the Holy Ghost in their lives.

❧ Pass around a notebook that travels from sister to sister during the lesson. Invite the sisters to each write one sentence that would be an effective way to begin a conversation with a less-active member. Read their entries at the end of the class.

❧ Create a PowerPoint presentation that includes photos of the sisters doing kind things to help less-active sisters in your ward. You could take pictures of the sisters before the lesson to show as part of your class, or you could create the PowerPoint during your lesson with pictures already taken as part of it and then share it next week, or even share it with the other auxiliaries in the ward. Instead of a PowerPoint, you could create a video.

❧ During the lesson, invite one of the sisters to draw your lesson on the chalkboard. She should illustrate what she hears the class talking about. You can rotate other sisters as artists every five minutes. It's always fun and entertaining to see what they draw!

Church Magazine Articles

❧ Silvia H. Allred, "Feed My Sheep," *Ensign*, November 2007.
❧ Ulisses Soares, "Feed My Sheep," *Ensign*, November 2005.
❧ James E. Faust, "Dear Are the Sheep That Have Wandered," *Ensign*, May 2003.
❧ Gordon B. Hinckley, "Find the Lambs, Feed the Sheep," *Ensign*, May 1999.
❧ Joseph B. Wirthlin, "Restoring the Lost Sheep," *Ensign*, May 1984.
❧ Robert D. Hales, "When Thou Art Converted, Strengthen Thy Brethren," *Ensign*, May 1997.

CHALLENGE

Look at your visiting teaching route to see if you have less-active sisters on your list and can step it up a notch. Ask the Relief Society president if there is a sister or two in the ward who need a new friend. Be that friend!

SEMINARY SCRIPTURE MASTERY

2 Nephi 32:3	Moroni 10:4–5
James 1:5–6	D&C 8:2–3
D&C 130:22–23	

PREACH MY GOSPEL

Pages 3, 18, 65, 89–93, 96–102

"Love engenders faith in Christ's plan of happiness, provides courage to begin the process of repentance, strengthens the resolve to be obedient to His teachings, and opens the door of service, welcoming in the feelings of self-worth and of being loved and needed."

Richard G. Scott, "We Love You—Please Come Back," *Ensign*, May 1986

"Love engenders faith in Christ's plan of happiness, provides courage to begin the process of repentance, strengthens the resolve to be obedient to His teachings, and opens the door of service, welcoming in the feelings of self-worth and of being loved and needed."

Richard G. Scott, "We Love You—Please Come Back," *Ensign*, May 1986

Lesson Thirteen
The Temple—The Great Symbol of Our Membership

. . . .

MUSIC

"God Is in His Holy Temple," *Hymns* #132
"High on the Mountain Top," *Hymns* #5
"Holy Temples on Mount Zion," *Hymns* #289
"How Beautiful Thy Temples, Lord," *Hymns* #288
"We Love Thy House, O God," *Hymns* #247

. . . .

SUMMARY

Sacred temples are built as a school for the Saints to receive eternal ordinances, make important covenants, and gain vital knowledge, all of which will bind their families together forever and allow them to enter into the celestial kingdom. Attending the temple is a symbol of our faithful membership in the Church. Prophets have encouraged us to get a temple recommend and use it as often as we can. Being "temple worthy" even when we don't live near a temple will allow us to become more like the Savior in thought and deed.

. . . .

QUOTES

"I think there is no place in the world where I feel closer to the Lord than in one of His holy temples" (Thomas S. Monson, "Blessings of the Temple," *Ensign*, October 2010).

"Attending the temple gives us a clearer perspective and a sense of purpose and peace" (Thomas S. Monson, "Blessings of the Temple," Temples, LDS.org).

"It is a place of peace, solitude, and inspiration. Regular attendance will enrich your life with greater purpose. It will permit you to provide deceased ancestors the exalting ordinances you have received. Go to the temple. You know it is the right thing to do. Do it now" (Richard G. Scott, "Receive the Temple Blessings," *Ensign*, May 1999).

"The Lord's work is one majestic work focused upon hearts, covenants, and priesthood ordinances" (David A. Bednar, "Missionary, Family History, and Temple Work," *Ensign*, October 2014).

"Always prayerfully express gratitude for the incomparable blessings that flow from temple ordinances. Live each day so as to give evidence to Father in Heaven and His Beloved Son of how very much those blessings mean to you" (Richard G. Scott, "Temple Worship: The Source of Strength and Power in Times of Need," *Ensign*, May 2009).

GOSPEL ART

Jesus Christ—(240 KIT, 1 GAB)
Boy Jesus in the Temple—(205 KIT, 34 GAB)
Jesus Cleansing the Temple—(224 KIT, 51 GAB)
My Father's House—(52 GAB)
Melchizedek Priesthood Restoration—(94 GAB)
Elijah Appearing in the Kirtland Temple—(95 GAB)
Kirtland Temple—(500 KIT, 117 GAB)
Nauvoo Illinois Temple—(501 KIT, 118 GAB)
Salt Lake Temple—(502 KIT, 119 GAB)
Young Couple Going to the Temple—(609 KIT, 120 GAB)
Temple Baptismal Font—(504 KIT, 121 GAB)
Temple Used Anciently—(118 KIT)
Elijah Restores the Power to Seal Families for Eternity—(417 KIT)
Washington DC Temple—(505 KIT)

VIDEOS

- "To Have Peace and Happiness": https://goo.gl/1wJrjz
- "Why Mormons Build Temples": https://goo.gl/R1TMce
- "Temples Are a Beacon": https://goo.gl/Yk3KaA
- "Temple Mirrors of Eternity": https://goo.gl/DiXzDE
- Mormon Messages: http://goo.gl/jAiuxy
- "Endowed with Power": https://goo.gl/YoiotB
- "The Blessings of the Temple": https://goo.gl/ofWLD6

Object Lessons

❧ Show the sisters several items (or pictures of items): candy, coins, dollar bills, stuffed animals, a diamond ring. Ask the class which item they think a baby would be most interested in. (Candy and toys.) Ask why the baby wouldn't select the most expensive item? (The baby doesn't understand the value of it.) Talk about how some people don't understand the value of temples, so they make choices that might prevent them from being worthy to enter the temple.

❧ Invite the sisters to share pictures of their favorite temple and faith-promoting stories about how the temple has blessed their lives.

❧ Access the Internet in your building and find some of the newer temples that are under construction or being remodeling by visiting them via Google Earth and Street Maps. Check out the new temples in Rome, Paris, and Provo!

❧ Invite someone in your ward who has recently attended the temple for the first time to talk about how he or she prepared and how the experience made him or her feel closer to the Savior. You can also invite some of the youth to share their experiences about going to the temple to do temple baptisms.

Church Magazine Articles

❧ Russell M. Nelson, "Prepare for Blessings of the Temple," *Ensign*, March 2002.

❧ David E. Sorensen, "The Doctrine of Temple Work," *Ensign*, October 2003.

❧ Howard W. Hunter, "A Temple-Motivated People," *Ensign*, February 1995.

❧ Stacy Vickery, "Temple Blessings Now and Eternally," *Ensign*, September 2011.

❧ Richard G. Scott, "Receive the Temple Blessings," *Ensign*, May 1999.

❧ Howard W. Hunter, "We Have a Work to Do," *Ensign*, March 1995.

🕊 Dennis B. Neuenschwander, "Bridges and Eternal Keepsakes," *Ensign*, May 1999.

● ●

CHALLENGE

Elder Richard G. Scott counseled us to make specific goals for attending the temple and to not let anything interfer with going. Encourage the sisters to set goals for temple attendance and to follow through with them. Elder Scott promised, "This pattern will guarantee that those who live in the shadow of a temple will be as blessed as are those who plan far ahead and make a long trip to the temple" ("How Can We Make the Most of Temple Attendance?" *New Era*, March 2012).

● ●

SEMINARY SCRIPTURE MASTERY

1 Corinthians 15:20–22   D&C 131:1–4

● ●

PREACH MY GOSPEL

Pages 31–32, 47–54, 85–86, 159–65

● ●

"Attending the temple gives us a clearer perspective and a sense of purpose and peace."

Thomas S. Monson, "Blessings of the Temple," LDS.org

"Attending the temple gives us a clearer perspective and a sense of purpose and peace."

Thomas S. Monson, "Blessings of the Temple," LDS.org

Lesson Fourteen
Hastening Family History
and Temple Work

• •

MUSIC

"Families Can Be Together Forever," *Hymns* #300
"God Is in His Holy Temple," *Hymns* #132
"High on the Mountain Top," *Hymns* #5
"Holy Temples on Mount Zion," *Hymns* #289
"How Beautiful Thy Temples, Lord," *Hymns* #288
"We Love Thy House, O God," *Hymns* #247

• •

SUMMARY

Salvation is given to every living man and woman, but exaltation requires that everyone be baptized and receive temple ordinances. For those who have lived on earth without hearing the gospel and receiving the saving ordinances, others can perform the temple work on their behalf. Our ancestors gave us the gift of life, and by doing their temple work, we can help them gain eternal life. A merciful Father in Heaven allows us to receive those ordinances for our ancestors who were not able to enter the temple for themselves and allows us to make eternal blessings available to them.

As we research our family's history to identify our ancestors, the Lord will help us. He wants families to be together and has given us the tools we need, as well as the sacred houses where they can be sealed. It is one of the most important works we can do here on earth. Our deceased loved ones are counting on us to help them with their eternal progression. If you want to have a spiritual experience, hasten your family history and temple work!

• •

QUOTES

"Genealogies, family stories, historical accounts, and traditions . . . form a bridge between past and future and bind generations together in ways that no other keepsake can" (Dennis B. Neuenschwander, "Bridges and Eternal Keepsakes," *Ensign*, May 1999).

"[The Lord] has trusted you by letting you hear the gospel in your lifetime, giving you the chance to accept the obligation to offer it to those of your ancestors who did not have your priceless opportunity. Think of the gratitude He has for those who pay the price in work and faith to find the names of their ancestors and who love them and Him enough to offer them eternal life in families, the greatest of all the gifts of God. He offered them an infinite sacrifice. He will love and appreciate those who paid whatever price they could to allow their ancestors to choose His offer of eternal life" (Henry B. Eyring, "Hearts Bound Together," *Ensign*, May 2005).

"There exists a righteous unity between the temple and the home. Understanding the eternal nature of the temple will draw you to your family; understanding the eternal nature of the family will draw you to the temple" (Gary E. Stevenson, "Sacred Homes, Sacred Temples," *Ensign*, May 2009).

"In the ordinances of the temple, the foundations of the eternal family are sealed in place" (Howard W. Hunter, "A Temple-Motivated People," *Ensign*, Febuary 1995).

GOSPEL ART

Boy Jesus in the Temple—(205 KIT, 34 GAB)
My Father's House—(52 GAB)
Elijah Appearing in the Kirtland Temple—(95 GAB)
Kirtland Temple—(500 KIT, 117 GAB)
Nauvoo Illinois Temple—(501 KIT, 118 GAB)
Salt Lake Temple—(502 KIT, 119 GAB)
Young Couple Going to the Temple—(609 KIT, 120 GAB)
Temple Baptismal Font—(504 KIT, 121 GAB)
Temple Used Anciently—(118 KIT)
Elijah Restores the Power to Seal Families for Eternity—(417 KIT)
Washington DC Temple—(505 KIT)
Adam and Eve Kneeling at an Altar—(4 GAB)
Adam and Eve Teaching Their Children—(5 GAB)
Jacob Blessing His Sons—(12 GAB)

VIDEOS

- "Eternal Family—Paul": https://goo.gl/JvHMYW
- "Temples Bless the Living and the Dead": https://goo.gl/1yRdWQ
- "RootsTech 2013 Family History Callings: First Hearts, Then Charts": https://goo.gl/e8Yw8m
- "Why Mormons Do Family History": https://goo.gl/gXQ1Ze

OBJECT LESSONS

- Have a talent contest to see who can comb their hair without bending their elbows. Ask two sisters to eat a candy bar without bending their elbows. What's the punch line? It can't be done, unless they help each other. Our ancestors need us as much as we needed them. Together, we save each other!
- Invite your ward family history specialist to share some special experiences about binding heaven with earth and explain how the family history library works.
- Get two large envelopes, one with a picture of a temple on the outside. Ask a volunteer to place paper dolls inside the two envelopes, representing families. Lick the envelope that has the picture of a temple on the outside. Talk about life's challenges that can tear us apart, and then turn the two envelopes upside down, shaking the contents around. The family that has been sealed together will stay together, but the dolls of the other family will all fall out of the envelope.

CHURCH MAGAZINE ARTICLES

- Dallin H. Oaks, "Family History: In Wisdom and in Order," *Ensign*, June 1989.
- David E Sorensen, "The Doctrine of Temple Work," *Ensign*, October 2003.
- Howard W. Hunter, "A Temple-Motivated People," *Ensign*, Febuary 1995.

- ❧ Stacy Vickery, "Temple Blessings Now and Eternally," *Ensign*, September 2011.
- ❧ Howard W. Hunter, "We Have A Work To Do," *Ensign*, March 1995.
- ❧ Dennis B. Neuenschwander, "Bridges and Eternal Keepsakes," *Ensign*, May 1999.

CHALLENGE

Watch the tutorial videos on the Church's new "Family Tree" website at FamilySearch.org. Click on "Family Tree" in the top menu. If you don't have one already, create an account and begin researching the names of your ancestors to see where you can begin doing their temple work.

SEMINARY SCRIPTURE MASTERY

1 Corinthians 15:20–22	D&C 131:1–4
2 Nephi 2:25	Moses 1:39
Genesis 1:26–27	Genesis 39:9
Exodus 20:3–17	

PREACH MY GOSPEL

Pages 31–32, 47–54, 85–86, 159–65

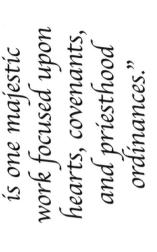

"*The Lord's work is one majestic work focused upon hearts, covenants, and priesthood ordinances.*"

David A. Bednar, "Missionary, Family History, and Temple Work," *Ensign*, October 2014

"*The Lord's work is one majestic work focused upon hearts, covenants, and priesthood ordinances.*"

David A. Bednar, "Missionary, Family History, and Temple Work," *Ensign*, October 2014

Lesson Fifteen
The Sacrament of the Lord's Supper

- -

MUSIC

"In Memory of the Crucified," *Hymns* #190
"While of These Emblems We Partake," *Hymns* #173 and #174
"He Died! The Great Redeemer Died," *Hymns* #192
"God Loved Us, So He Sent His Son," *Hymns* #187
"Again We Meet around the Board," *Hymns* #186
"Father in Heaven, We Do Believe," *Hymns* #180
"We'll Sing All Hail to Jesus' Name," *Hymns* #182

- -

SUMMARY

The sacrament is an ordinance designed by the Lord to help us remember His atoning sacrifice and the hope we have in Him of returning to live with our Father in Heaven. It is full of rich symbolism and offers an opportunity to renew our baptismal covenants, which also incorporate the same symbols.

The bread represents the Savior's body, which was ransomed for us on the cross and later resurrected in glory. The wine (water) causes our mind to reflect on the blood that was shed for our sins, by which we are atoned for our sins. By partaking of the sacrament each week at church, we are remembering our covenants and that through Christ, we too can overcome physical and spiritual death.

When the bread and water trays are placed on the table at church with the white tablecloth carefully draped over them, they symbolically represent Christ on the cross, and later the linen-covered body in the tomb. The sacrament is a powerful image of the Atonement of Jesus Christ.

- -

QUOTES

"The Spirit heals and renews our souls. The promised blessing of the sacrament is that we will 'always have his Spirit to be with [us]'" (Cheryl A. Esplin, "The Sacrament—A Renewal for the Soul," *Ensign*, November 2014).

"When we partake of the sacrament with a sincere heart, with real intent, forsaking our sins, and renewing our commitment to God, the Lord provides a way whereby sins can be forgiven" (Vaughn J. Featherstone, "Sacrament Meeting and the Sacrament," *Ensign*, September 2001).

"As we worthily partake of the sacrament, we will sense those things we need to improve in and receive the help and determination to do so. No matter what our problems, the sacrament always gives hope" (John H. Groberg "The Beauty and Importance of the Sacrament," *Ensign*, May 1989).

"Reminding us weekly of our need to foster charity toward our fellow Saints, the sacrament can be a great force for unity in our congregations" (John S. Tanner, "Reflections on the Sacrament Prayers," *Ensign*, April 1986).

"[As we partake of the sacrament,] . . . our witness that we are willing to take upon us the name of Jesus Christ constitutes our declaration of candidacy for exaltation in the celestial kingdom" (Dallin H. Oaks, "Taking upon Us the Name of Jesus Christ," *Ensign*, May 1985).

- -

GOSPEL ART

Jesus Washing the Apostles' Feet—(226 KIT, 55 GAB)
Jesus Praying in Gethsemane—(227 KIT, 56 GAB)
The Crucifixion—(230 KIT, 57 GAB)
Burial of Jesus—(232 KIT, 58 GAB)
Mary and the Resurrected Lord—(233 KIT, 59 GAB)
Jesus Shows His Wounds—(234 KIT, 60 GAB)
Jesus at the Door—(237 KIT, 65 GAB)
The Resurrected Jesus Christ—(239 KIT, 66 GAB)
Jesus Christ—(240 KIT, 1 GAB)
The Empty Tomb—(245 KIT)

Blessing the Sacrament—(603 KIT, 107 GAB)
Passing the Sacrament —(604 KIT, 108 GAB)

• •

Videos

🎞 "Sacrament of the Lord's Supper": https://goo.gl/Ap6qth
🎞 "Sacredness of the Sacrament": https://goo.gl/vUkMcQ
🎞 "The Emblems of the Sacrament": https://goo.gl/Y9pv28
🎞 "The Sacrament—A Renewal for the Soul": https://goo.gl/mmSIJB
🎞 "Sacrament Worship": https://goo.gl/HcrT0b

• •

Object Lessons

🎞 Prepare a pane of clear glass or picture frame that is dirty on one side and show it to the class. Sometimes we don't even realize how dirty we're getting from the world (inside and out) because it accumulates over time. Use a glass cleaner to clear away some of the dirt on the glass. By going to church and partaking of the sacrament, we can become unspotted from the world and have clearer vision. Read Doctrine and Covenants 59:9 to the class.
🎞 Pass out a basket with four different kinds of candy in it. After the sisters have selected their candy, divide them into four groups based on which type of candy they selected. Each group will then be given a different topic to discuss:
   • What do you do to help you focus on the Savior during sacrament meeting?
   • How do you help your children keep the Sabbath Day holy and make the sacrament meaningful to them?
   • How do you prepare to take the sacrament before the meeting starts?
   • What do you do to "always remember Him" during the week?
🎞 Sing one verse from each of the suggested hymns for this lesson. Music always invites the Spirit into a room in such a beautiful way.

⁊ Invite some of the young men in the ward who have taken the sacrament to home-bound members to share their experiences about that loving act of service.

• •

CHURCH MAGAZINE ARTICLES

⁊ L. Tom Perry, "As Now We Take the Sacrament," *Ensign*, May 2006.

⁊ Dallin H. Oaks, "Sacrament Meeting and the Sacrament," *Ensign*, November 2008

⁊ Russell M. Nelson, "Worshipping at Sacrament Meeting," *Ensign*, August 2004.

⁊ David B. Haight, "The Sacrament—and the Sacrifice," *Ensign*, April 2007.

⁊ David B. Haight, "Remembering the Savior's Atonement," *Ensign*, April 1988

• •

CHALLENGE

Pass out cards for the sisters to write down things they want to think about during the sacrament. Offer suggestions for quotes or scriptures they could write on their cards. Encourage them to refer to those cards next Sunday when the sacrament is being passed.

• •

SEMINARY SCRIPTURE MASTERY

2 Nephi 32:8–9	Mosiah 3:19
Isaiah 1:18	Isaiah 53:3–5
John 3:5	John 14:15
John 17:3	1 Corinthians 15:20–22
D&C 19:16–19	D&C 58:42–43

• •

PREACH MY GOSPEL

Pages 9, 63–64, 74

• •

"*The Spirit heals and renews our souls. The promised blessing of the sacrament is that we will 'always have his Spirit to be with [us].'*"

Cheryl A. Esplin, "The Sacrament—a Renewal for the Soul," *Ensign*, November 2014

"*The Spirit heals and renews our souls. The promised blessing of the sacrament is that we will 'always have his Spirit to be with [us].'*"

Cheryl A. Esplin, "The Sacrament—a Renewal for the Soul," *Ensign*, November 2014

Lesson Sixteen
Marriage—An Eternal Partnership

. . . .

MUSIC

"Home Can Be a Heaven on Earth," *Hymns #298*
"I Am a Child of God," *Hymns #301*
"O My Father," *Hymns #292*
"Teach Me to Walk in the Light," *Hymns #304*

. . . .

SUMMARY

Marriage is ordained of God and is between a man and a woman. Temple marriage is a sacred partnership with God and is essential for exaltation, which is the perfect union of man and woman. Temple marriage is a covenant partnership with the Lord that allows us to seal souls together as eternal families.

Celestial marriage is the crowning ordinance of the gospel of Jesus Christ. The benefits of a temple marriage not only are eternal but also bless our mortal life together. Joy in marriage grows sweeter as husband and wife both remain faithful and obedient gospel covenants.

Be sensitive to the sisters in the class who may have lost a spouse, been divorced, or never married. Remind them the Lord has promised a fulness of blessings to all those who are faithful.

. . . .

QUOTES

"To those who keep the covenant of marriage, God promises the fulness of His glory, eternal lives, eternal increase, exaltation in the celestial kingdom, and a fulness of joy" (F. Burton Howard, "Eternal Marriage," *Ensign,* May 2003).

"Marriage between a man and a woman is ordained of God, and only through the new and everlasting covenant of marriage can we realize the fulness of all eternal blessings" (David E. Sorensen, "The Honeymoon Trail," *Liahona,* October 1997, 16–19).

93

"Temple marriage is a covenant that bridges death, transcends time, stretches unbreakable into eternity" (Spencer W. Kimball, "Temples and Eternal Marriage," *Ensign*, August 1974, 2–6).

· ·

GOSPEL ART

Adam and Eve Kneeling at an Altar—(4 GAB)
Adam and Eve Teaching Their Children—(5 GAB)
Jacob Blessing His Sons—(12 GAB)
Lehi's Dream—(69 GAB)
Elijah Appearing in the Kirtland Temple—(95 GAB)
Young Couple Going to the Temple—(120 GAB)

· ·

VIDEOS

❧ "Come Follow Me: Marriage and Family" (There are a bunch on this page): http://goo.gl/zmuNtF
❧ "Eternal Marriage": https://goo.gl/iBKVCJ

· ·

OBJECT LESSONS

❧ Have two sisters hold a short string across the front the room, one on each end. Now ask another sister to attach a clothespin to the string, except give her only half of a clothespin. She won't be able to attach it. Give her a complete clothespin and allow her to attach it to the string. Now ask another sister to cut the string with scissors; however, give her only half of the scissors. She won't be able to complete the task. Now give her a real pair of scissors and allow her to cut the string.

Both items serve as great analogies for marriage. If only one person is trying to hang on, it won't work; you need both partners to work together. Likewise, if both partners in the marriage choose "cutting" remarks and are always fighting, it won't take long for everything to fall apart.

❧ Have a husband and wife play pretend tug-of-war using a paper chain. The chain represents civil marriage. It doesn't take long to separate if husband and wife are pulling at opposite ends with different goals. If the chain isn't strong, it won't take much for it to break. Now ask the same husband and wife play tug-of-war using a metal chain, which represents temple marriage. With a strong foundation, even if the couple struggles through life, they can hold the marriage together.

❧ Hold up a donut and compare it to temporal marriage. It's sweet and delicious but built around a big hole: " 'til death do us part." Tell the sisters, " 'Do-nut' settle for a marriage that won't last into the eternities." Pass around cinnamon rolls, comparing those to eternal marriage without a hole.

· ·

CHURCH MAGAZINE ARTICLES

❧ Spencer W. Kimball, "The Importance of Celestial Marriage," *Ensign*, October 1979, 2–6.

❧ Bruce C. Hafen, "Covenant Marriage," *Ensign*, November 1996, 26–28.

❧ F. Burton Howard, "Eternal Marriage," *Ensign*, May 2003, 92–94.

❧ Spencer W. Kimball, "Temples and Eternal Marriage," *Ensign*, August 1974, 2–6.

❧ Marion D. Hanks, "Eternal Marriage," *Ensign*, November 1984.

❧ L. Whitney Clayton, "Marriage: Watch and Learn," *Ensign*, May 2013.

· ·

CHALLENGE

If you are married, write a list of all the good qualities you see in your spouse. Refer to this list when you get frustrated with him. Choose one new act of service you will perform for him this week that you've never done before.

If you have never been married, pray for patience. Look online for a singles conference you could attend and invite some friends to attend with you. If you are an older widow, pray for comfort until you and your spouse can be reunited. Discover ways you can use your talents to bless others.

· ·

Seminary Scripture Mastery

2 Nephi 2:25	Moses 1:39
Genesis 1:26–27	Genesis 39:9
Exodus 20:3–17	D&C 131:1–4

• •

Preach My Gospel

Pages 3, 31, 47–50, 54, 85–86, 159–60, 163–65

• •

"We also believe that strong traditional families are not only the basic units of a stable society, a stable economy, and a stable culture of values—but that they are also the basic units of eternity and of the kingdom and government of God."

L. Tom Perry, "Why Marriage and Family Matter— Everywhere in the World," *Ensign*, May 2015

"We also believe that strong traditional families are not only the basic units of a stable society, a stable economy, and a stable culture of values—but that they are also the basic units of eternity and of the kingdom and government of God."

L. Tom Perry, "Why Marriage and Family Matter— Everywhere in the World," *Ensign*, May 2015

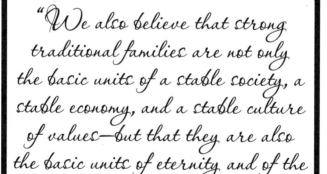

Lesson Seventeen
Preserve and Protect the Family

. . . .

MUSIC

"Families Can Be Together Forever," *Hymns* #300
"Home Can Be a Heaven on Earth," *Hymns* #298
"I Am a Child of God," *Hymns* #301
"O My Father," *Hymns* #292
"Our Father, by Whose Name," *Hymns* #296
"Teach Me to Walk in the Light," *Hymns* #304

. . . .

SUMMARY

Life is eternal. We come from heavenly parents, who are waiting for us to return to them, having learned the lessons of life and gained the characteristics they possess. To remind us of our heavenly home, we are given the opportunity to be parents here on earth and raise a family of our own. Exaltation is a family affair. The family is the most important unit in time and eternity.

Heavenly Father has placed us here on earth in families so that we can learn to work together and help one another return to our heavenly home, each one playing an important role. Fathers are to provide, protect, and preside over families. Mothers are divinely designed to bear and nurture children. Children are commanded to honor and obey their parents. If everyone takes responsibility for a happy family, they can all experience a little bit of heaven on earth.

Be sensitive to the sisters in the class who may have lost a spouse, divorced, or never married. Remind them the Lord has promised a fulness of blessings to all those who are faithful.

. . . .

QUOTES

"The entire theology of our restored gospel centers on families and on the new and everlasting covenant of marriage" (L. Tom Perry,

"Why Marriage and Family Matter—Everywhere in the World," *Ensign*, May 2015).

"There exists a righteous unity between the temple and the home. Understanding the eternal nature of the temple will draw you to your family; understanding the eternal nature of the family will draw you to the temple" (Gary E. Stevenson, "Sacred Homes, Sacred Temples," *Ensign,* May 2009, 102).

"In light of the ultimate purpose of the great plan of happiness, I believe that the ultimate treasures on earth and in heaven are our children and our posterity" (Dallin H. Oaks, "The Great Plan of Happiness," *Ensign,* November 1993).

"Under the plan of heaven, the husband and the wife walk side by side as companions, neither one ahead of the other, but a daughter of God and a son of God walking side by side. Let your families be families of love and peace and happiness. Gather your children around you and have your family home evenings, teach your children the ways of the Lord, read to them from the scriptures, and let them come to know the great truths of the eternal gospel as set forth in these words of the Almighty" (Gordon B. Hinckley, "Latter-Day Counsel: Selections from Addresses of President Gordon B. Hinckley," *Ensign,* March 2001, 64).

"Our family is the focus of our greatest work and joy in this life; so will it be throughout all eternity" (Russell M. Nelson, "Set in Order Thy House," *Ensign,* November 2001).

"In the ordinances of the temple, the foundations of the eternal family are sealed in place" (Howard W. Hunter, "A Temple-Motivated People," *Ensign,* February 1995).

"We also believe that strong traditional families are not only the basic units of a stable society, a stable economy, and a stable culture of values—but that they are also the basic units of eternity and of the kingdom and government of God" (L. Tom Perry, "Why Marriage and Family Matter—Everywhere in the World," *Ensign,* May 2015).

"The key to strengthening our families is having the Spirit of the Lord come into our homes. The goal of our families is to be on the straight and narrow path" (Robert D. Hales, "Strengthening Families: Our Scred Duty," *Ensign,* May 1999).

Gospel Art

Adam and Eve Kneeling at an Altar—(4 GAB)
Adam and Eve Teaching Their Children—(5 GAB)
Jacob Blessing His Sons—(12 GAB)
Lehi's Dream—(69 GAB)
Elijah Appearing in the Kirtland Temple—(95 GAB)
Young Couple Going to the Temple—(120 GAB)

Videos

- "Faith and Families": https://goo.gl/Ytg68m
- "Home and Family": https://goo.gl/AtavkA
- "Protect Our Nestlings": https://goo.gl/RopmKn
- There is a collection of short video clips called "Family Conversations" you can choose from to meet the needs of your sisters: https://goo.gl/ior7J9
- "Proclamation": https://goo.gl/UakubZ

Object Lessons

- Pass out copies of the family proclamation for everyone in the class and have them color and decorate them during your lesson.
- Place a stalk of celery in a glass of colored water a few days prior to your lesson. The food coloring in the water will actually be drawn up into the celery! Show the class your visual aid and ask them to draw analogies between the celery and food coloring and our parenting skills. Children literally soak up what is around them in the home: anger, love, gospel study, apathy. We need to constantly expose our children to positive behaviors in order for them to absorb the gospel.
- Show the sisters a beautiful rose. Have the sisters get into groups of four to answer the following questions:
  - What is a rose that is currently blooming in your family life? (Something you're enjoying.)
  - What is a thorn that is currently challenging you in your family life? (Something that is a struggle.)

- What is a bud you would like to work on? (Something good in your family that hasn't bloomed yet and requires work on your part.)

❧ Play four corners to get to know the sisters and their families better. Identify which corners of the room will be represented by A, B, C, and D. Feel free to make up more fun questions! Invite the sisters to stand in the corner of the room that corresponds to the answer they most relate to.

- How many people do you have in your family?
  - A. 1–2
  - B. 3–4
  - C. 5–6
  - D. 7–10
- What stage of education is happening in your family now?
  - A. Elementary school
  - B. Middle school
  - C. High school
  - D. College
- What activities does your family love to do the most?
  - A. Activities with sports
  - B. Activities with dancing
  - C. Activities with water
  - D. Activities with an electronic device
- What kind of food does your family love the most?
  - A. Homemade cooking
  - B. Anything that can be eaten in the car
  - C. Fancy schmancy restaurants
  - D. Anything on a party table
- Where does your family get the most spiritual strength?
  - A. Reading the scriptures together
  - B. Praying together
  - C. Attending the temple together
  - D. Going to church together

Church Magazine Articles

❧ Robert D. Hales, "The Eternal Family," *Ensign*, November 1996.

ક Henry B. Eyring, "The Family," *Ensign*, February 1998.

ક L. Tom Perry, "The Importance of the Family," *Ensign*, May 2003.

ક Spencer W. Kimball, "Living the Gospel in the Home," *Ensign*, May 1978.

ક Carol B. Thomas, "Strengthen Home and Family," *Ensign*, May 2002.

ક Joanne B. Doxey, "Strengthening the Family," *Ensign*, November 1987.

CHALLENGE

Write down the names of everyone in your family. List things you can do to serve them and help them reach their personal goals this month.

SEMINARY SCRIPTURE MASTERY

Ether 12:27

D&C 58:26–27

D&C 131:1–4

Moroni 7:45, 47–48

D&C 88:124

PREACH MY GOSPEL

Pages 47–59, 85–86

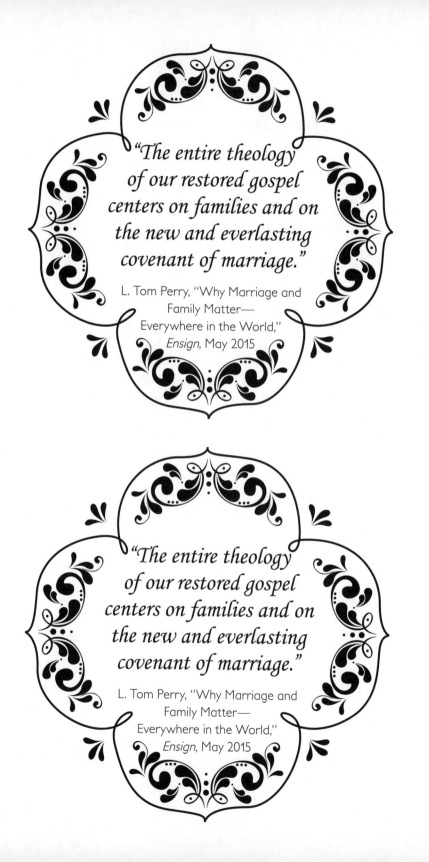

"The entire theology
of our restored gospel
centers on families and on
the new and everlasting
covenant of marriage."

L. Tom Perry, "Why Marriage and
Family Matter—
Everywhere in the World,"
Ensign, May 2015

"The entire theology
of our restored gospel
centers on families and on
the new and everlasting
covenant of marriage."

L. Tom Perry, "Why Marriage and
Family Matter—
Everywhere in the World,"
Ensign, May 2015

Lesson Eighteen
We Believe in Being Honest

. . . .

Music

"Father in Heaven, We Do Believe," *Hymns* #180
"I Believe in Being Honest," *Children's Songbook* #149
"Improve the Shining Moments," *Hymns* #226
"The Thirteenth Article of Faith," *Children's Songbook* #132
"A Prayer," *Children's Songbook* #22

. . . .

Summary

Religion isn't just something we believe; it's truly the blueprint for how we live our daily lives. We believe in being honest with others and with God. The gospel of Jesus Christ isn't about learning interesting scriptural facts or debating doctrine, but rather, it is about applying those principles to our behavior and becoming Christlike in all that we say and do. Heavenly Father cares more about who we are and what we are becoming than what we know.

Integrity is doing what you know to be true. Hypocrisy is when we go to church one day and act like nonbelievers the other six days of the week. We can't live worldly lives and then expect heavenly rewards. As members of the Church, we are expected to learn the gospel, live it, and share it. It should be our goal to progress from knowing to doing and becoming.

. . . .

Quotes

"From the beginning to the end of His ministry, Jesus asked His followers to adopt new, higher standards in contrast to their former ways. As believers, they were to live by a spiritual and moral code that would separate them not only from the rest of the world, but also even from some of their traditions. He asks nothing less of those who follow Him today" (David B. Haight, "Ethics and Honesty," *Ensign*, November 1987).

"As disciples of the Savior, we are not merely striving to know more; rather, we need to consistently do more of what we know is right and become better. We should remember that bearing a heartfelt testimony is only a beginning. We need to bear testimony, we need to mean it, and most importantly we need consistently to live it. We need to both declare and live our testimonies" (David A. Bednar, "More Diligent and Concerned at Home," *Ensign,* November 2009).

"Where there is honesty, other virtues will follow" (Gordon B. Hinckley, "An Honest Man—God's Noblest Work," *Ensign*, May 1976).

"Honesty is more than not lying. It is truth telling, truth speaking, truth living, and truth loving" (James E. Faust, "Honesty—A Moral Compass," *Ensign*, November 1996).

"As God condemns immorality, so he denounces hypocrisy, which is one of the worst forms of dishonesty" (Mark E. Petersen, "Honesty, a Principle of Salvation," *Ensign*, December 1971).

GOSPEL ART

Enoch and His People Are Taken up to God—(120 KIT, 6 GAB)
Sermon on the Mount—(212 KIT, 39 GAB)
Jesus Christ (240 KIT, 1 GAB)
King Benjamin Addresses His People (307 KIT, 74 GAB)
The Anti-Nephi-Lehies Burying Their Swords (311 KIT)
The Articles of Faith (618 KIT)
My Gospel Standards (619 KIT)

VIDEOS

- "Honesty: You Better Believe It!": https://goo.gl/gtlECm
- "Honesty, Trust, Integrity": https://goo.gl/gIMkU8
- "Teachings of Gordon B. Hinckley: Standing for Something": https://goo.gl/67CTr9
- "Honesty": https://goo.gl/KFtxNI

OBJECT LESSONS

- Pass out blank bingo boards to everyone and invite the sisters to write their own words in each square, using words that have to do with honesty and integrity from the lesson manual. Tell them that whenever you say one of the words on their boards, they can put a marker on that square. Markers could be small candies. As soon as a sister has marked a straight line either vertically, horizontally, or diagonally, she can call out "bingo" and collect a prize. You can play during the entire lesson, allowing several sisters to win.

- Divide the sisters into small groups to make up their own parables that illustrate the importance of being honest and having integrity. Invite them to share their parables with the rest of the class.

- Have you ever attended BYU's annual Women's Conference in May? While sisters attend classes on a variety of topics during two days, their busy hands make thousands of items that are later donated to children in need around the world. Go to the link to see twenty-one service projects and crafts that were done this last year: https://goo.gl/ltO4nV. Your Relief Society may want to adopt a project to work on during a month of Sunday lessons. They are adorable, meaningful, and fun!

. . . .

CHURCH MAGAZINE ARTICLES

- David B. Haight, "Ethics and Honesty," *Ensign*, November 1987.
- Mark E. Petersen, "Honesty, a Principle of Salvation," *Ensign*, December 1971.
- James E. Faust, "Honesty—A Moral Compass," *Ensign*, November 1996.
- Delbert L. Stapley, "Honesty and Integrity," *Ensign*, June 1971.
- Quentin L. Cook, "Let There Be Light!" *Ensign*, November 2010.
- Gordon B. Hinckley, "An Honest Man—God's Noblest Work," *Ensign*, May 1976.

. . . .

CHALLENGE

Write a list of ways you can be more honest with yourself and others. What lies are you telling yourself to rationalize bad behavior? How can you improve your integrity with others?

SEMINARY SCRIPTURE MASTERY

1 Nephi 3:7
Moroni 7:45, 47–48
1 Samuel 16:7
Luke 24:36–39
2 Timothy 3:15–17
D&C 88:124

Mosiah 4:30
Exodus 20:3–17
Psalm 24:3–4
John 14:15
D&C 64:9–11
D&C 121:36, 41–42

PREACH MY GOSPEL

Pages 19, 66, 72, 76, 88, 122–26, 168–69

"*From the beginning to the end of His ministry, Jesus asked His followers to adopt new, higher standards in contrast to their former ways. As believers, they were to live by a spiritual and moral code that would separate them not only from the rest of the world but also even from some of their traditions. He asks nothing less of those who follow Him today.*"

David B. Haight, "Ethics and Honesty," *Ensign*, November 1987

"*From the beginning to the end of His ministry, Jesus asked His followers to adopt new, higher standards in contrast to their former ways. As believers, they were to live by a spiritual and moral code that would separate them not only from the rest of the world but also even from some of their traditions. He asks nothing less of those who follow Him today.*"

David B. Haight, "Ethics and Honesty," *Ensign*, November 1987

"*From the beginning to the end of His ministry, Jesus asked His followers to adopt new, higher standards in contrast to their former ways. As believers, they were to live by a spiritual and moral code that would separate them not only from the rest of the world but also even from some of their traditions. He asks nothing less of those who follow Him today.*"

David B. Haight, "Ethics and Honesty," *Ensign*, November 1987

Lesson Nineteen
Our Commitment to God

MUSIC

"Come, We That Love the Lord," *Hymns* #119
"O Love That Glorifies the Son," *Hymns* #295
"God Is Love," *Hymns* #87
"Because God Loves Me," *Children's Songbook* #234
"Seek the Lord Early," *Children's Songbook* #108
"Keep the Commandments," *Hymns* #303

SUMMARY

Most of us would say that we love God. How do we show Him our sincere love and gratitude? The answer is simple: by doing His will and keeping His commandments (see John 14:15). There are two great commandments: love God and love our fellowman. The order of those mandates is significant. If we truly love God, everything else will fall into its proper order. The blessings we receive by loving God will help us to love and bless our fellowman.

God is a loving Heavenly Father who formed this earth as a school for our learning and progression. We need to believe in God, but we also need to do His will, despite what others do. We are not only His greatest creation but His sons and daughters. By keeping His commandments and serving others, we can become like Him and return to live with Him.

QUOTES

"True happiness is not made in getting something. True happiness is becoming something. This can be done by being committed to lofty goals. We cannot become something without commitment" (Marvin J. Ashton, "The Word Is Commitment," *Ensign*, November 1983).

"Love is the measure of our faith, the inspiration for our obedience, and the true altitude of our discipleship" (Dieter F. Uchtdorf, "The Love of God," *Ensign*, November 2009).

"To love God with all your heart, soul, mind, and strength is all-consuming and all-encompassing. It is no lukewarm endeavor. It is total commitment of our very being" (Ezra Taft Benson, "The Great Commandment—Love the Lord," *Ensign*, May 1988).

"We have got to reach a higher plane: we have got to love God more than we love the world" (Lorenzo Snow, *Teachings of the Presidents of the Church: Lorenzo Snow* [The Church of Jesus Christ of Latter-day Saints, 2011]).

GOSPEL ART

The Brother of Jared Sees the Finger of the Lord—(318 KIT, 85 GAB)
Three Men in the Fiery Furnace—(116 KIT, 25 GAB)
Daniel in the Lions' Den—(117 KIT, 26 GAB)
Abinadi before King Noah—(308 KIT, 75 GAB)
Samuel the Lamanite on the Wall—(314 KIT, 81 GAB)
Joseph Smith in Liberty Jail—(97 GAB)
Building the Ark—(102 KIT, 7 GAB)
Noah and the Ark with Animals—(103 KIT, 8 GAB)
Daniel Refusing the King's Meat and Wine—(114 KIT, 23 GAB)
Enoch and His People Are Taken up to God—(120 KIT, 6 GAB)
Calling of the Fishermen—(209 KIT, 37 GAB)
Christ and the Rich Young Ruler—(244 KIT, 48 GAB)
The Anti-Nephi-Lehies Burying Their Swords—(311 KIT)
Boy Samuel Called by the Lord—(111 KIT, 18 GAB)
John the Baptist Baptizing Jesus—(208 KIT, 35 GAB)
Christ Ordaining the Apostles—(211 KIT, 38 GAB)
Lehi's Family Leaving Jerusalem—(301 KIT)
Alma Baptizes in the Waters of Mormon—(309 KIT, 76 GAB)

VIDEOS

- "The Two Great Commandments": https://goo.gl/UOJhfA
- "Put God First": https://goo.gl/OfWgEb

- "I Will Give Myself to Him": https://goo.gl/XeXLiV
- "Obedience": https://goo.gl/OW7RW5
- "The Greatest Commandment": http://goo.gl/8SIoGY

. . . .

OBJECT LESSONS

- Pass out some baby food jars filled with whipping cream. Tell the class to shake the jars if they love the Lord. Explain that we show the Lord how much we really do love Him by the way we live and the things we do. Love is an action! Have the class shake the jars during the lesson until the cream turns into sweet butter. Before the lesson ends, pass out blueberry muffins that the butter can be served on for all to enjoy, because living the gospel is *sweet*!

- Begin by showing a padlock and ask what it can be used for. Ask what good a lock is without a key. Discuss how our lives only find meaning in relationship with our Creator. God has made us and this earth for a purpose. Jesus Christ is the key. Life without God is like a padlock without a key.

- Ask, "How many of you would like to see God?" Pass around a mirror and discuss how each one of us is made in His image and is truly divine. We can see God's reflection in Jesus. To see God clearly, we need to follow the Savior and His example and serve others.

- Scramble up letters to words using this fun online tool: http://goo.gl/oMYgXy. Try words like oancdmemstmn (commandments) or ipisoetrir (priorities). Have the class try to figure out the words. Later, explain that even if we can disguise our true character from the world, the Lord sees who we really are. Our goal is to become like Him.

. . . .

CHURCH MAGAZINE ARTICLES

- Rex C. Reeve, "Look to God," *Ensign*, November 1982.
- Robert F. Orton, "The First and Great Commandment," *Ensign*, November 2001.
- Dieter F. Uchtdorf, "The Love of God," *Ensign*, November 2009.

❧ Gordon B. Hinckley, "In These Three I Believe," *Ensign*, July 2006.

❧ Bernard P. Brockbank, "Knowing God," *Ensign*, July 1972.

- -

CHALLENGE

Create a to-do list of things you need to accomplish this week. Put them into two categories: ways you love God and ways you love others. Where are you spending the majority of your time and energy?

- -

SEMINARY SCRIPTURE MASTERY

1 Nephi 3:7	2 Nephi 32:3
Helaman 5:12	Moroni 10:4–5
Exodus 20:3–17	Joshua 24:15
Proverbs 3:5–6	John 14:15
John 17:3	2 Thessalonians 2:1–3
D&C 19:16–19	

- -

PREACH MY GOSPEL

Pages 5–7, 31–32, 36–37, 48, 66, 72, 76

- -

"True happiness is not made in getting something. True happiness is becoming something. This can be done by being committed to lofty goals. We cannot become something without commitment."

Marvin J. Ashton, "The Word Is Commitment," *Ensign*, November 1983

"True happiness is not made in getting something. True happiness is becoming something. This can be done by being committed to lofty goals. We cannot become something without commitment."

Marvin J. Ashton, "The Word Is Commitment," *Ensign*, November 1983

"True happiness is not made in getting something. True happiness is becoming something. This can be done by being committed to lofty goals. We cannot become something without commitment."

Marvin J. Ashton, "The Word Is Commitment," *Ensign*, November 1983

"True happiness is not made in getting something. True happiness is becoming something. This can be done by being committed to lofty goals. We cannot become something without commitment."

Marvin J. Ashton, "The Word Is Commitment," *Ensign*, November 1983

Lesson Twenty
Walking the Savior's Path of Charity

. . . .

MUSIC

"A Poor Wayfaring Man of Grief," *Hymns* #29

"As Sisters in Zion," *Hymns* #309

"Because I Have Been Given Much," *Hymns* #219

"I Have Work Enough to Do," *Hymns* #224

"Sweet Is the Work," *Hymns* #317

"Love One Another," *Children's Songbook* #136

. . . .

SUMMARY

How can you tell a true disciple of Jesus Christ? By the way she treats other people! One way we show the Lord how much we love Him is by serving His children, our brothers and sisters. When we feel God's love deep inside our souls, we feel a desire to reach outside ourselves and bless others. A true understanding of the gospel of Jesus Christ compels us to love and serve.

If we want to be like Christ, we need to do as Christ did: serve others. The Savior ministered daily to the needs of those around Him. When we open our spiritual eyes, we will see many opportunities around us for Christlike service and love. The act of serving others helps the Lord accomplish His work and makes us more like Him. The Lord uses us to bless those around us.

Charity is the pure love of Christ and the greatest of all virtues. Charity cannot be developed in the abstract; it requires clinical, hands-on experience. It is a process, not an event. The more we serve others, the more genuine our love will become for them.

Introduce the sisters in your Relief Society to several great websites they can visit with their families to choose service projects in their area and reach out to others in their community:

❧ www.servenet.org

❧ www.idealist.org

114

- www.serve.gov
- www.volunteers.com
- www.nationalservice.gov

. . . .

QUOTES

"We learn that charity, though often quantified as the action, is actually the state of the heart that prompts us to love one another" (Elaine L. Jack "Strengthened in Charity," *Ensign*, November 1996).

"I am convinced that true brotherly love is essential to our happiness and to world peace. . . . We need to show our love, beginning in the home and then widening our circle of love to encompass our ward members, our less active and nonmember neighbors, and also those who have passed beyond the veil" (Jack H Goaslind Jr., "Reach Out to Our Father's Children," *Ensign*, May 1981).

"Charity is not just a precept or a principle, nor is it just a word to describe actions or attitudes. Rather, it is an internal condition that must be developed and experienced in order to be understood" (C. Max Caldwell, "Love of Christ," *Ensign*, November 1992).

"When you get the Spirit of God . . . you feel full of kindness, charity, long-suffering, and you are willing all the day long to accord to every man that which you want yourself" (John Taylor, *Teachings of the Presidents of the Church: John Taylor* [The Church of Jesus Christ of Latter-day Saints, 2011]).

"The more we serve our fellowmen in appropriate ways, the more substance there is to our souls" (Spencer W. Kimball, "Small Acts of Service," *Ensign*, December 1974).

. . . .

GOSPEL ART

Jesus Christ—(240 KIT, 1 GAB)
City of Zion is Taken Up—(120 KIT, 6 GAB)
Christ Healing the Sick at Bethesda—(42 GAB)
The Good Samaritan—(44 GAB)
Jesus Washing the Apostles' Feet—(226 KIT, 55 GAB)
Jesus Praying in Gethsemane—(227 KIT, 56 GAB)
Jesus Carrying a Lost Lamb—(64 GAB)

King Benjamin Addresses His People—(307 KIT, 74 GAB)
Ammon Defends the Flocks of King Lamoni—(310 KIT, 78 GAB)
Jesus Healing the Nephites—(317 KIT, 83 GAB)
The Foundation of the Relief Society—(98 GAB)
The Sermon on the Mount—(212 KIT, 39 GAB)
Jesus Blesses the Nephite Children—(84 GAB)
Service—(115 GAB)

VIDEOS

- "David Andre Koch, Feed My Sheep": https://goo.gl/fcn750
- "Feed My Lambs": https://goo.gl/DQphzx
- "Being a More Christian Christian": https://goo.gl/dZ9Kku
- "Ye Have Done It unto Me": https://goo.gl/glUf5C

OBJECT LESSONS

- Show a set of silverware and ask the sisters to describe their different functions:
  - Fork—stabs the item with an attitude of "This is mine!"
  - Knife—cuts everything to be a different size or separate it
  - Spoon—gathers small things together
  Which kind of service do you want to give? Make me a spoon!
- Teach the sisters how to knit or crochet so that during your lesson they can begin making leper bandages to send to the Church's Humanitarian Center. You'll find tons of things your Relief Society can do to serve at www.ldsphilanthropies.org. Items can be sent to

      LDS Philanthropies
      15 E. South Temple
      2nd Floor East
      Salt Lake City, UT 84150
      Telephone: (801) 240-5567

- At the beginning of your lesson, remove your shoes, earrings, and other accessories or easily removable clothing, without explaining why. (Be modest!) At the end of the lesson say, "You probably won't remember a word I said by the time you get home, but you will never forget what I did at the beginning of the lesson. Actions speak louder than words." We can talk about being Christlike, but when we serve we truly are Christlike.

- Pass around a mirror and ask the sisters to look in it. Ask them if they were able to see anyone else when they focused on their own image? (No.) By serving others, we focus less on our own problems and challenges and gain improved perspective.
- Make "Friendship Fudge" during the lesson by passing around gallon-size bags of ingredients that the sisters have to squish together to form the sweet treat.

Recipe:
- 4 cups powdered sugar
- 3 ounces softened cream cheese
- ½ cup softened margarine
- ½ cup cocoa
- 1 tsp. vanilla
- ½ cup chopped nuts

When it is mixed together, roll it into a log, slice it, and serve.

CHURCH MAGAZINE ARTICLES

- Henry B. Eyring, "Feeding His Lambs," *Ensign*, February 2008.
- Derek A. Cuthbert, "The Spirituality of Service," *Ensign*, May 1990.
- Jeffery R. Holland, " 'Charity Never Faileth': A Discussion on Relief Society," *Ensign*, March 2011.
- V. Dallas Merrell, "A Vision of Service," *Ensign*, December 1996.
- Spencer W. Kimball, "Small Acts of Service," *Ensign*, December 1974.
- Russell C. Taylor, "The Joy of Service," *Ensign*, November 1984.
- Gene R. Cook, "Charity: Perfect and Everlasting Love," *Ensign*, May 2002.

CHALLENGE

Talk to your Relief Society president or compassionate service leader to see what you can do to serve. Who needs help in your ward? Your service can be anonymous or performed by your entire family.

● ●

SEMINARY SCRIPTURE MASTERY

2 Nephi 28:7–9   Mosiah 2:17
Moroni 7:45, 47–48   Moses 7:18
D&C 64:9–11   D&C 88:124

● ●

PREACH MY GOSPEL

Pages 1–2, 8, 87, 115, 118, 122–26, 168–69

● ●

"We learn that charity, though often quantified as the action, is actually the state of the heart that prompts us to love one another."

Elaine L. Jack, "Strengthened in Charity," *Ensign*, November 1996

"We learn that charity, though often quantified as the action, is actually the state of the heart that prompts us to love one another."

Elaine L. Jack, "Strengthened in Charity," *Ensign*, November 1996

"We learn that charity, though often quantified as the action, is actually the state of the heart that prompts us to love one another."

Elaine L. Jack, "Strengthened in Charity," *Ensign*, November 1996

"We learn that charity, though often quantified as the action, is actually the state of the heart that prompts us to love one another."

Elaine L. Jack, "Strengthened in Charity," *Ensign*, November 1996

Lesson Twenty-One
Faith and Testimony

. . . .

MUSIC

"Go Forth with Faith," *Hymns* #263
"Faith of Our Fathers," *Hymns* #84
"When Faith Endures," *Hymns* #128
"True to the Faith," *Hymns* #254
"Come unto Jesus," *Hymns* #117

. . . .

SUMMARY

The first principle of the gospel is faith in the Lord Jesus Christ. Faith is believing in Him with our spiritual eyes when we haven't seen Him with our physical eyes. It is a principle of action that compels us to pray, repent, be obedient, and trust in His promises. We increase our faith by testing and studying His words. Faith has power to move mountains, accomplish miracles, and prove us worthy to see God.

As we exercise faith in the Lord, live His commandments, and pray for understanding, we gain a testimony. Elder Dallin H. Oaks described a testimony as "a personal witness borne to our souls by the Holy Ghost that certain facts of eternal significance are true and that we know them to be true" ("Testimony," *Ensign*, May 2008). As we live gospel principles, we test them in our lives and gain knowledge that they are true and have blessed our lives.

. . . .

QUOTES

"Honestly acknowledge your questions and your concerns, but first and forever fan the flame of your faith, because all things are possible to them that believe" (Jeffery R. Holland, "Lord, I Believe," *Ensign*, May 2013).

"It is not enough to know that God lives, that Jesus Christ is our Savior, and that the gospel is true. We must take the high road by acting upon that knowledge" (Dallin H. Oaks, "Be Not Deceived," *Ensign*, November 2004).

"This is my prayer for all of us—'Lord, increase our faith.' Increase our faith to bridge the chasms of uncertainty and doubt. . . . Grant us faith to look beyond the problems of the moment to the miracles of the future. . . . Give us faith to do what is right and let the consequence follow" (Gordon B. Hinckley, "Lord, Increase Our Faith," *Ensign*, November 1987).

"We promote the process of strengthening our faith when we do what is right—increased faith always follows" (L. Whitney Clayton, "Help Thou Mine Unbelief," *Ensign*, November 2001).

"Faith in Jesus Christ takes us beyond mere acceptance of the Savior's identity and existence. It includes having complete confidence in His infinite and eternal redemptive power" (James O. Mason, "Faith in Jesus Christ," *Ensign,* April 2001).

GOSPEL ART

Jesus Praying in Gethsemane—(227 KIT, 56 GAB)
The Crucifixion—(230 KIT, 57 GAB)
Jesus at the Door—(237 KIT, 65 GAB)
The Resurrected Jesus Christ—(239 KIT)
Jesus Christ—(240 KIT, 1 GAB)
Enos Praying—(305 KIT, 72 GAB)
The Anti-Nephi-Lehies Burying Their Swords—(311 KIT)
Conversion of Alma the Younger—(321 KIT, 77 GAB)
The Ten Commandments—(14 GAB)
Abraham Taking Isaac to be Sacrificed—(105 KIT, 9 GAB)
Three Men in the Fiery Furnace—(116 KIT, 25 GAB)
Daniel in the Lions' Den—(117 KIT, 26 GAB)
Moses and the Brass Serpent—(123 KIT, 16 GAB)
Christ Healing a Blind Man—(213 KIT, 42 GAB)
Jesus Raising Jairus's Daughter—(215 KIT, 41 GAB)
Two Thousand Young Warriors—(313 KIT, 80 GAB)
The Brother of Jared Sees the Finger of the Lord—(318 KIT, 85 GAB)
The Articles of Faith—(618 KIT)

VIDEOS

- "The Transforming Power of Faith and Character," Richard G. Scott: https://goo.gl/62IK94
- "We Believe: Theme Song": https://goo.gl/0k9YVQ
- *Finding Faith in Christ*: https://goo.gl/ezxTnF
- "Waiting on Our Road to Damascus": http://goo.gl/fXEQzR

OBJECT LESSONS

- At the end of this book is a list of websites where you can get free clip art. Create a family home evening packet about faith and testimony that sisters can copy and take home to use with their families. Invite sisters to color pictures and cut out visual aids for their packet while they listen to the lesson. Provide scissors, crayons, and markers.
- Show the class a checkerboard with one grain of wheat on the first square, two on the second, four on the third, and continue doubling it every square. Ask the class, "At this rate of doubling every square, how much grain would you have on the checkerboard by the time you reach the sixty-fourth square?" Let the class guess and then tell them the correct answer is enough grain to cover the entire subcontinent of India fifty feet deep! Each square represents some area of their lives where they need to trust God. Talk about how our faith may start out small, but as God uses it, the end result can be miraculous and quite powerful.
- Ask someone to lift objects of various weights. Some objects should be light and easy to lift, and others should be quite difficult to lift. Ask the sisters what they could do to help the sister lifting without touching her weights. Ask how building faith is like building muscle. Talk about what kind of learning could be done to strengthen faith. Ask how our faith can help us lift our heavy burdens in life. Compare the light weights with leisure learning; contrast that with the heavier weights, which represent true study of topics. We need to combine deeper study with our daily reading strengthen our faith.

Church Magazine Articles

❧ Gordon B. Hinckley, "Faith: The Essence of True Religion," *Ensign*, October 1995.

❧ Russell M. Nelson, "Faith in Jesus Christ," *Ensign*, March 2008.

❧ Robert D. Hales, "Finding Faith in the Lord Jesus Christ," *Ensign*, November 2004.

❧ Robert D. Hales, "Strengthening Faith and Testimony," *Ensign*, November 2013

❧ Henry B. Eyring, "Testimony and Conversion," *Ensign*, February 2015.

Challenge

Write a list of all the things that build your faith. Begin doing one of the things on your list that you haven't included in your daily life.

Seminary Scripture Mastery

2 Nephi 2:27	2 Nephi 28:7–9
Mosiah 4:30	Alma 32:21
Alma 41:10	Ether 12:6
Genesis 39:9	Exodus 20:3–17
Psalm 24:3–4	Proverbs 3:5–6
Isaiah 1:18	John 14:15
James 1:5–6	James 2:17–18
D&C 19:16–19	D&C 58:42–43
D&C 82:10	

Preach My Gospel

Pages 50, 61–63, 93–95, 155, 187–90

"Honestly acknowledge your questions and your concerns, but first and forever fan the flame of your faith, because all things are possible to them that believe."

Jeffrey R. Holland, "Lord, I Believe," *Ensign*, May 2013

"Honestly acknowledge your questions and your concerns, but first and forever fan the flame of your faith, because all things are possible to them that believe."

Jeffrey R. Holland, "Lord, I Believe," *Ensign*, May 2013

"Honestly acknowledge your questions and your concerns, but first and forever fan the flame of your faith, because all things are possible to them that believe."

Jeffrey R. Holland, "Lord, I Believe," *Ensign*, May 2013

"Honestly acknowledge your questions and your concerns, but first and forever fan the flame of your faith, because all things are possible to them that believe."

Jeffrey R. Holland, "Lord, I Believe," *Ensign*, May 2013

Lesson Twenty-Two
Teaching the Gospel

. . . .

MUSIC

"Help Me Teach With Inspiration," *Hymns* #281
"How Will They Know?" *Children's Songbook* #182
"We'll Bring the World His Truth (Army of Helaman),"
Children's Songbook #172
"Come, All Whose Souls Are Lighted," *Hymns* #268
"Go, Ye Messengers of Glory," *Hymns* #262

. . . .

SUMMARY

Because the Lord knows we learn the most when we teach and serve others, we are often called to teach gospel classes at church. In the spirit of love and inspiration, we are to build faith and invite others to Christ. The most important part of effective teaching is not our carefully chosen words but the spirit with which we teach. This is the Lord's work, and sharing the gospel is one of the most important things we can do here on earth.

As members of the Church, it is our privilege and duty to share the knowledge of life and salvation that we have been blessed with. We are commanded to keep the commandments and then teach them to others. When we do, our joy will be felt for eternity. The Lord entrusts us with this important work, and it is our privilege to be a part of it.

. . . .

QUOTES

"Successful gospel teachers love the gospel. They are excited about it. And because they love their students, they want them to feel as they feel and to experience what they have experienced. To teach the gospel is to share your love of the gospel" (David M. McConkie, "Gospel Learning and Teaching," *Ensign*, November 2010).

"Our teaching will be effective if we approach it humbly through prayer and study" (L. Tom Perry, "Teach Them the Word of God with All Diligence," *Ensign*, May 1999).

"No other teaching talent can compensate for lack of the Spirit. Why is that? Because it is the Spirit that builds faith, it is the Spirit that softens hearts, it is the Spirit that enlightens minds, and it is the Spirit that brings about conversion" (Tad R. Callister, "5 Ways to Become a 'Teacher Come from God,'" *Church News*, July 21, 2015).

"The First Presidency has said that one of the threefold missions of the Church is to proclaim the gospel. If we accept this mission, we should be willing to center our efforts on bringing souls unto the Lord on condition of repentance. . . . In talking of faith and saving souls, you should understand that when the Spirit is present, people are not offended when you share your feelings about the gospel" (M. Russell Ballard, "We Proclaim the Gospel," *Ensign*, November 1986).

"After all that has been said, the greatest and most important duty is to preach the Gospel" (Joseph Smith, *History of the Church*, 2:478).

- -

GOSPEL ART

Boy Jesus in the Temple—(205 KIT, 34 GAB)
John Preaching in the Wilderness—(207 KIT)
Calling of the Fishermen—(209 KIT, 37 GAB)
Mary and Martha—(219 KIT, 45 GAB)
Go Ye Therefore—(235 KIT, 61 GAB)
Abinadi before King Noah—(308 KIT, 75 GAB)
Jesus Christ—(240 KIT, 1 GAB)
Adam and Eve Teaching Their Children—(GAB 5)
Lehi Prophesying to the People of Jerusalem—(GAB 67)
King Benjamin Addresses His People—(GAB 74)
Jesus Teaching in the Western Hemisphere—(GAB 82)
The Gift of the Holy Ghost—(GAB 105)

- -

VIDEOS

ॐ "Love Those You Teach": https://goo.gl/RC8lAH
ॐ "Teach the Doctrine": https://goo.gl/FqQESA

🕸 "Loving and Serving Others": https://goo.gl/WKUc2D
🕸 "Find, Take, Teach": https://goo.gl/YTHKHR
🕸 "The Heart and a Willing Mind": https://goo.gl/Xv9gha

OBJECT LESSONS

🕸 Use the suggested scriptures in the manual for this lesson. Toss out three balls or bean bags to the class. On one ball, tape a strip of paper that says "Scripture." On another ball, tape a strip of paper that says "Context." On the last ball, tape a strip of paper that says "Practical Application." The sister that catches the "Scripture" ball reads the assigned scripture aloud. The sister that catches the "Context" ball provides some history about when that scripture was given and under what circumstances. The sister who catches the "Practical Application" ball shares ideas on how we can apply that scriptural advice to our lives, specifically on how we can improve our teaching.

🕸 Pair up the sisters to answer some of the questions in the "Suggestions for Study and Teaching" section of the manual. Ask one of the questions and give one sister in each pair exactly sixty seconds to answer it to her partner. Ask another question and give the other sister sixty seconds to answer. After two questions, have all of the sisters switch partners and ask them two more questions. Rotate pairs until all of the questions have been asked.

🕸 Invite seminary and Primary teachers to speak to your class about creative teaching techniques they have used with teens and small children to make learning fun.

🕸 Divide the class into small groups. Assign each group a different gospel principle and have them create an object lesson for it, such as the Holy Ghost, repentance, missionary work, tithing, or baptism. After a few minutes of brainstorming, invite the group to present their idea to the class. Talk about why object lessons are so effective in helping learners understand and remember concepts better.

🕸 Choose one of the seminary scripture mastery verses listed below that correlate with this lesson's topic and teach the sisters different techniques to memorize it. Encourage them to help their kids memorize the seminary verses too! You can find memorization ideas at http://goo.gl/o1WOMx.

• •

Church Magazine Articles

- "Who, Me? Teach?" *Ensign*, January 2010.
- Dallin H. Oaks, "Sharing the Gospel," *Ensign*, November 2001.
- David B. Haight, "Teach One Another," *Ensign*, June 1971.
- L. Tom Perry, "Teach Them with the Word of God with All Diligence," *Ensign,* May 1999.
- Tad R. Callister, "5 Ways to Become a 'Teacher Come from God,'" *Church News*, July 21, 2015.

• •

Challenge

If you have a calling to teach in the Church, read *Teaching, No Greater Call* and make a list of five specific things you can do to improve your teaching. You can access it at https://goo.gl/FydRGP.

• •

Seminary Scripture Mastery

2 Nephi 9:28–29	2 Nephi 32:8–9
Mosiah 2:17	Alma 37:35
Abraham 3:22–23	Proverbs 3:5–6
Isaiah 29:13–14	Ephesians 4:11–14
2 Timothy 3:15–17	James 1:5–6
D&C 18:10, 15–16	D&C 89:18–21
D&C 130:122–23	

• •

Preach My Gospel

Pages 1–3, 8, 18–24, 38, 71, 82, 92, 96–102, 175–78, 180–86, 190–92, 195–99

• •

"*Successful gospel teachers love the gospel. They are excited about it. And because they love their students, they want them to feel as they feel and to experience what they have experienced. To teach the gospel is to share your love of the gospel.*"

David M. McConkie, "Gospel Learning and Teaching," *Ensign*, November 2010

"*Successful gospel teachers love the gospel. They are excited about it. And because they love their students, they want them to feel as they feel and to experience what they have experienced. To teach the gospel is to share your love of the gospel.*"

David M. McConkie, "Gospel Learning and Teaching," *Ensign*, November 2010

"*Successful gospel teachers love the gospel. They are excited about it. And because they love their students, they want them to feel as they feel and to experience what they have experienced. To teach the gospel is to share your love of the gospel.*"

David M. McConkie, "Gospel Learning and Teaching," *Ensign*, November 2010

"*Successful gospel teachers love the gospel. They are excited about it. And because they love their students, they want them to feel as they feel and to experience what they have experienced. To teach the gospel is to share your love of the gospel.*"

David M. McConkie, "Gospel Learning and Teaching," *Ensign*, November 2010

Lesson Twenty-Three
"No Less Serviceable"

MUSIC

"Put Your Shoulder to the Wheel," *Hymns #252*
"Come, Come, Ye Saints," *Hymns #30*
"Have I Done Any Good?" *Hymns #223*
"I Have Work Enough to Do," *Hymns #224*
"Improve the Shining Moments," *Hymns #226*
"Let Us All Press On," *Hymns #243*

SUMMARY

We are commanded to be anxiously engaged in good works, especially those activities that build the Lord's kingdom here on earth. The Lord has organized His Saints into wards and stakes so that we can serve one another, have leadership opportunities, and be gathered into safety. We don't have to have a high-profile calling to offer valuable service and make meaningful contributions.

Our wards and stakes help us become unified with one another and perfected as we love and serve. Like tent stakes that are secured firmly into the ground, our Church stakes are to anchor us to the Savior and His earthly kingdom, providing a refuge from the world and a school wherein we can practice living the gospel. Why and how we serve in the Church is more important than where we serve.

QUOTES

"We must not allow ourselves to focus on the fleeting light of popularity or substitute that attractive glow for the substance of true but often anonymous labor that brings the attention of God, even if it does not get coverage on the six o'clock news" (Howard W. Hunter, "No Less Serviceable," *Ensign,* April 1992).

"Service is an imperative for those who worship Jesus Christ. To followers who were vying for prominent positions in his kingdom, the

Savior taught, 'Whosoever will be chief among you, let him be your servant,'" (Dallin H. Oaks, "Why Do We Serve?" *Ensign*, November 1984).

"I see two kinds of service: one, the service we render when we are called to serve in the Church; the other, the service we willingly give to those around us because we are taught to care" (Boyd K. Packer, "Called to Serve," *Ensign*, November 1997).

GOSPEL ART

Ruth Gleaning in the Fields—(17 GAB)
Building the Ark—(102 KIT, 7 GAB)
Calling of the Fishermen—(209 KIT, 37 GAB)
The Good Samaritan—(218 KIT, 44 GAB)
Go Ye Therefore—(235 KIT, 61 GAB)
Jesus Carrying a Lost Lamb—(64 GAB)
Jesus at the Door—(237 KIT, 65 GAB)
Lehi's Dream—(69 GAB)
Captain Moroni Raises the Title of Liberty—(312 KIT, 79 GAB)
Two Thousand Young Warriors—(313 KIT, 80 GAB)
The Foundation of the Relief Society—(98 GAB)
Service—(115 GAB)

VIDEOS

- "Beautiful Zion, Built Above": https://goo.gl/1LzwaQ
- "Unto All the World: The Stone Cut Out of the Mountain": https://goo.gl/Ublts4
- "I Will Go and Do": https://goo.gl/Vtkxzx

OBJECT LESSONS

- Bring a weight or heavy barbell to the class and ask one sister to lift it. (Choose a sister who you think won't be able to.) Now ask several sisters to come help her. Together, they will be able to do it easily. Talk about how we have the blessing of callings where we can help each other accomplish the tasks and commandments the Lord has given us.

❧ Before class, put a five-dollar bill in someone's scriptures without her noticing. (Choose someone who is a good sport and who won't be leaving during the lesson!) During the lesson, ask the sister to bring her scriptures up to the front of class to help you with something. Ask her, "Do you know me as a friend and trust me? Do you think that I would lie to you? If I gave you a very simple task that you could accomplish right up here with me, would you do it?" After she answers, tell her, "Give me five dollars." She will be flustered and won't feel as though she can help you. Reach for her scriptures and take the five-dollar bill out. Explain that God will never give us a task that He has not already given us the talents and ability to accomplish. We may not see them at first, but He has put them there. We must ask for His help and strength in doing His will. The Lord gives us callings to build our faith and abilities.

❧ Divide the sisters into generational chat groups: young and single, young mothers, middle-aged women, and "golden oldies." Have each group talk about callings they have held in the Church and lessons they have learned during their service. Each group could answer one of the questions listed at the end of the lesson in the manual under "Suggestions for Study and Teaching."

• •

Church Magazine Articles

❧ Harold B. Lee, "Strengthen the Stakes of Zion," *Ensign*, July 1973.

❧ Dallin H. Oaks, "Why Do We Serve?" *Ensign*, November 1984.

❧ Bruce R. McConkie, "Come: Let Israel Build Zion," *Ensign*, May 1977.

❧ Boyd K. Packer, "Called to Serve," *Ensign*, November 1997.

• •

Challenge

Write a letter to people in your ward who serve quietly and valiantly, thanking them for the service they perform for your ward members. Offer to help set up or clean up after the next ward or stake event.

• •

SEMINARY SCRIPTURE MASTERY

Moses 7:18   Abraham 3:22–23
Matthew 16:15–19   Ephesians 4:11–14

• •

PREACH MY GOSPEL

Pages 3, 5, 83, 108, 115, 179, 213–21

• •

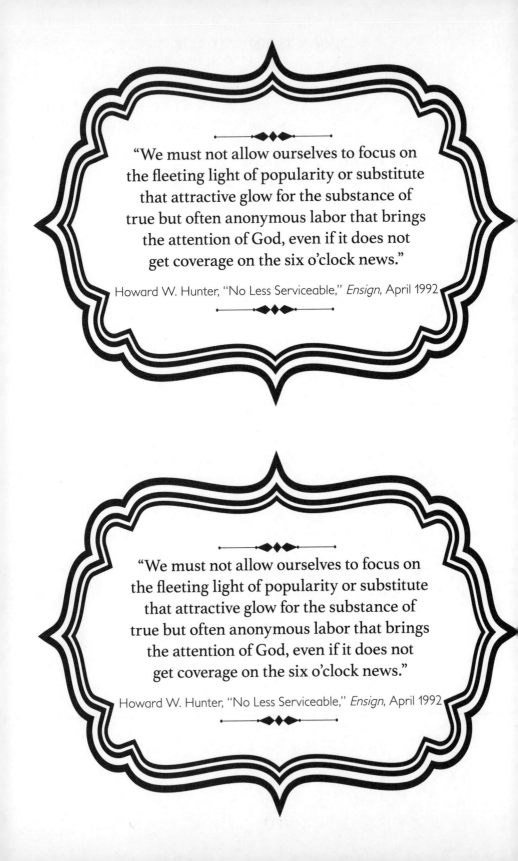

"We must not allow ourselves to focus on the fleeting light of popularity or substitute that attractive glow for the substance of true but often anonymous labor that brings the attention of God, even if it does not get coverage on the six o'clock news."

Howard W. Hunter, "No Less Serviceable," *Ensign*, April 1992

"We must not allow ourselves to focus on the fleeting light of popularity or substitute that attractive glow for the substance of true but often anonymous labor that brings the attention of God, even if it does not get coverage on the six o'clock news."

Howard W. Hunter, "No Less Serviceable," *Ensign*, April 1992

Lesson Twenty-Four
Following the Example
of Jesus Christ

· ·

MUSIC

"I Know That My Redeemer Lives," *Hymns* #136
"Jesus, Lover of My Soul," *Hymns* #102
"I'm Trying to Be Like Jesus," *Children's Songbook* #78
"The Lord Is My Light," *Hymns* #89
"Jesus, the Very Thought of Thee," *Hymns* #141
"Come unto Jesus," *Hymns* #117

· ·

SUMMARY

What is at the center of our daily lives? More to the point, *who* is our life centered on? Our challenge during mortality is to choose the eternal kingdom of God rather than temporary earthly glory. What good is the Atonement if you don't follow in Christ's footsteps?

As this is the last lesson of 2016, it might be nice to take some time during the lesson to have the sisters reflect on all of the lessons they received during the year and how those lessons helped them come closer to Christ. What changes did they make in their lives to focus more on the Savior? What experiences strengthened their testimonies? What goals could they set for 2017 to become more Christlike in their thoughts, words, and actions?

· ·

QUOTES

"Following Christ is not a casual or occasional practice, but a continuous commitment and way of life that applies at all times and in all places" (Dallin H. Oaks, "Followers of Christ," *Ensign*, May 2013).

"The Christ-centered life produces in us, not a woeful countenance, but a disciplined enthusiasm to work righteousness" (Neal A. Maxwell, "The Christ-Centered Life," *Ensign*, August 1981).

"I bear witness that obedience to the gospel plan is the only way to build a Christ-centered life" (Merrill J. Bateman, "Living a Christ-Centered Life," *Ensign*, January 1999).

"In this, the dispensation of the fulness of time, as we prepare for the final satanic battles in anticipation of the return of Christ to the earth, it is very important to know who is on the Lord's side. The Lord needs to know on whom He can rely" (Robert C. Oaks, "Who's on the Lord's Side? Who?" *Ensign*, May 2005).

"If you will remain on the Lord's side of the line, the adversary cannot come there to tempt you" (Charles W. Dahlquist II, "Who's on the Lord's Side?" *Ensign,* May 2007).

"The Lord has left no doubt in defining His side and where the Saints should be in their thoughts, words, actions, and practices. We have His counsel in the scriptures and in the words of the prophets" (Joseph B. Wirthlin, "The Lord's Side," *Ensign,* March 1993).

"To follow Christ is to become more like Him. It is to learn from His character. As spirit children of our Heavenly Father, we do have the potential to incorporate Christlike attributes into our life and character" (Dieter F. Uchtdorf, "Developing Christlike Attributes," *Ensign*, October 2008).

• •

GOSPEL ART

Daniel in the Lions' Den—(117 KIT, 26 GAB)
Enoch and His People Are Taken Up to God—(120 KIT, 6 GAB)
Calling of the Fishermen—(209 KIT, 37 GAB)
Jesus Washing the Apostles' Feet—(226 KIT, 55 GAB)
Jesus at the Door—(237 KIT, 65 GAB)
Christ and the Rich Young Ruler—(244 KIT, 48 GAB)
Alma Baptizes in the Waters of Mormon—(309 KIT, 76 GAB)
The Anti-Nephi-Lehies Burying Their Swords—(311 KIT)
Captain Moroni Raises the Title of Liberty—(312 KIT, 79 GAB)
Two Thousand Young Warriors—(313 KIT, 80 GAB)
Salt Lake Temple—(503 KIT, 119 GAB)
Baptism—(601 KIT, 103 and 104 GAB)
Young Boy Praying—(605 KIT, 111 GAB)
Family Prayer—(606 KIT, 112 GAB)

Young Couple Going to the Temple—(609 KIT, 120 GAB)
Search the Scriptures—(617 KIT)
Boy Jesus in the Temple—(205 KIT, 34 GAB)
Childhood of Jesus Christ—(206 KIT)
John the Baptist Baptizing Jesus—(208 KIT, 35 GAB)
Go Ye Therefore—(235 KIT, 61 GAB)
The Second Coming—(238 KIT, 66 GAB)
The Resurrected Jesus Christ—(239 KIT)
Jesus Teaching in the Western Hemisphere—(315 KIT, 82 GAB)
Christ and Children from around the World—(608 KIT)
Jesus Blesses the Nephite Children—(84 GAB)

VIDEOS

- "What Is Discipleship?": https://goo.gl/9LqG3I
- "Reflections on a Consecrated Life": https://goo.gl/8Rm8Ww
- "Choose This Day": https://goo.gl/699Dlo
- "Answers to Life's Great Questions": https://goo.gl/bVuI1G

OBJECT LESSONS

- Get a picture of Jesus Christ where He is in the center and other items or people are surrounding him. Cut it up into puzzle pieces and invite the sisters to put it together. Notice that once you put Christ in the center, the rest of the picture puzzle is easier to solve.
- Show various pictures of items that represent sources of light: sun, solar panel, flashlight, candle, porch light, spotlight, lighthouse, fireplace, nightlight. Talk about their unique purposes and then show a picture of the Savior. Compare and contrast what His purpose is to the objects you discussed. How can we follow His example in our lives?
- This lesson will be given during the Christmas season, so you can sing Christmas carols, reenact the Nativity story, share family Christmas traditions, or prepare gifts for others, all while talking about how we can keep Christ at the center of our lives all year long. You can also talk about the symbols of Christmas that

point us to Christ and share ideas on how we can surround our-selves with items in our home to remind us to stay centered on the Savior.

• •

CHURCH MAGAZINE ARTICLES

- ❧ Richard J. Maynes, "Establishing a Christ-Centered Home," *Ensign*, May 2011.
- ❧ Lawrence E. Corbridge, "Valiant in the Testimony of Jesus Christ," *Ensign*, September 2011.
- ❧ Clate W. Mask Jr., "Standing Spotless before the Lord," *Ensign*, May 2004.
- ❧ Stephen A. West, "Are You on the Lord's Side?" *New Era*, Septtember 2002.
- ❧ Bernard P. Brockbank, "Knowing God," *Ensign*, July 1972.
- ❧ N. Eldon Tanner, "A Basis for Faith in the Living God," *Ensign*, November 1978.

• •

CHALLENGE

Look at the list of Christlike qualities that are included on page 126 of *Preach My Gospel*. Evaluate how you are doing in developing those characteristics. Create a plan of action for how you will make Christ more central in your daily thoughts and actions.

• •

SEMINARY SCRIPTURE MASTERY

2 Nephi 32:3	Helaman 5:12
Moroni 10:4–5	Exodus 20:3–17
Joshua 24:15	Proverbs 3:5–6
Isaiah 53:3–5	Luke 24:36–39
John 14:15	John 17:3
Ephesians 4:11–14	Revelation 20:12–13
D&C 76:22–24	Joseph Smith—History 1:15–20

• •

PREACH MY GOSPEL

Pages 1, 5–6, 32–33, 36–37, 48, 51–54, 60–62, 90, 105, 108, 115–16, 123–26, 198–99

• •

"*Following Christ is not a casual or occasional practice but a continuous commitment and way of life that applies at all times and in all places.*"

Dallin H. Oaks, "Followers of Christ,"
Ensign, May 2013

"*Following Christ is not a casual or occasional practice but a continuous commitment and way of life that applies at all times and in all places.*"

Dallin H. Oaks, "Followers of Christ,"
Ensign, May 2013

"*Following Christ is not a casual or occasional practice but a continuous commitment and way of life that applies at all times and in all places.*"

Dallin H. Oaks, "Followers of Christ,"
Ensign, May 2013

Website Resources

No need to reinvent the wheel, especially when you're using that wheel to drive on the information super highway! The Internet has an endless resource of ideas, recipes, downloads, crafts, lesson material, music, and instructions for almost anything you'd like to do in your Relief Society Sunday lessons.

Allow me to give you a serious word of caution about doing online searches. If you enter "women" into a search engine, you will get suggestions for links to all kinds of horrible pornographic websites. You must type in "LDS women" or "Relief Society," and even then, look at the description of the site before you click on it!

LDS Website Resources

- LDS.org (The official website of The Church of Jesus Christ of Latter-day Saints. This should be your first stop on the web.)
- www.jennysmith.net
- www.theideadoor.com
- www.mormons.org
- www.mormonfind.com
- www.lightplanet.com/mormons
- www.ldsworld.com
- www.JeanniGould.com
- www.sugardoodle.net
- www.ldssplash.com
- www.ldstoday.com

Merchandise

- www.ldscatalog.com (Church Distribution Center to order materials)
- www.byubookstore.com
- www.ldsliving.com
- www.deseretbook.com
- www.ctr-ring.com
- http://booksandthings.com/

LDS Relief Society Blogs

- enrichmentideas.blogspot.com
- thereliefsocietyblog.blogspot.com
- www.hollyscorner.com/blog/lds-resources/relief-society/
- www.mormonmomma.com/index.php/category/church/relief-society/
- www.families.com/lds
- segullah.org/daily-special/putting-the-relief-in-relief-society/

Internet Groups

I highly recommend that you join a Relief Society Yahoo group. It's free to join, and you'll meet some of the nicest people around! People share helpful ideas and tips in a real-time setting. You can receive the emails individually or as a daily digest. Some groups are more active than others, so the quantity of emails will vary. No reason to stress when another great Relief Society teacher has already done it out there somewhere!

- http://groups.yahoo.com/group/ReliefSociety-L/
- http://uk.groups.yahoo.com/group/Relief_SocietyLDS/
- http://groups.yahoo.com/group/ldsreliefsocietypresidency/
- http://groups.yahoo.com/group/LDSReliefSocietyMeetings/

Clip Art

I'm thankful for talented artists who share their wonderful creations with me, since I have trouble drawing decent stick people! Most of the websites above have pictures as well as these generous artists:

- www.graphicgarden.com
- designca.com/lds/
- www.coloringbookfun.com
- www.stums.org/closet/html/index.html
- www.oneil.com.au/lds/pictures.html
- http://goo.gl/2ACLAk (LDS images on About.com)
- www.free-clip-art.net

- www.coloring.ws/coloring.html
- www.apples4theteacher.com

• •

Music

- www.lds.org/music
- www.mormonchannel.org
- www.lds.org/youth/music
- yourldsmusicstore.com
- www.defordmusic.com
- www.ldsmusicworld.com
- www.ldsmusicsource.com
- www.ldspianosolo.com
- www.deseretbook.com/LDS-Music/
  Sheet-Music-Downloads/s/1395

About the Author

Trina Boice grew up in California and currently lives in Las Vegas, where she teaches at the famous Le Cordon Bleu School for Culinary Arts. You can see her yummy pictures on Instagram! In 2004, she was honored as the California Young Mother of the Year, an award that completely amuses her four sons. She earned two bachelor's degrees from BYU, where she competed on the speech and debate team and the ballroom dance team. She was president of the National Honor Society Phi Eta Sigma and served as ASBYU secretary of Student Community Services. She currently teaches online for BYU–I.

Trina also studied at the University of Salamanca in Spain and later returned there to serve an LDS mission in Madrid for a year and a half. She has a real estate license, travel agent license, two master's degrees, and a black belt in Tae Kwon Do, although she's the first one to admit that she'd pass out from fright if she were ever really attacked by a bad guy.

ABOUT THE AUTHOR

She worked as a legislative assistant for a congressman in Washington, DC, and was given the Points of Light Award and Presidential Volunteer Service Award for her domestic and international community service. She wrote a column called "The Boice Box" for a newspaper in Georgia, where she lived for fifteen years. She taught Spanish at a private high school and ran an appraisal business with her husband for twenty years. She currently writes for several newspapers and websites.

Trina was selected by KPBS in San Diego to be a political correspondent during the last presidential election. If she told you what she really did, she'd have to kill you.

A popular and entertaining speaker, Trina is the author of more than eighteen books with another one hitting stores soon!

Check out her movie reviews at www.MovieReviewMaven.blogspot.com and author blog at www.BoiceBox.blogspot.com.